BASIC ILLUSTRATED

Edible Wild Plants and Useful Herbs

Help Us Keep This Guide Up to Date

Every effort has been made by the author and editors to make this guide as accurate and useful as possible. However, many things can change after a guide is published. We would appreciate hearing from you concerning your experiences with this guide and how you feel it could be improved and kept current. While we may not be able to respond to all comments and suggestions, we'll take them to heart, and we'll also make certain to share them with the author. Please send your comments and suggestions to the following email address: editorial@GlobePequot.com.

Thanks for your input, and happy identifying!

BASIC ILLUSTRATED
Edible Wild Plants and Useful Herbs

Third Edition

Jim Meuninck

ESSEX, CONNECTICUT

An imprint of Globe Pequot, the trade division of
The Rowman & Littlefield Publishing Group, Inc.
4501 Forbes Blvd., Ste. 200
Lanham, MD 20706
www.rowman.com

Falcon and FalconGuides are registered trademarks and Make Adventure Your Story is a trademark of The Rowman & Littlefield Publishing Group, Inc.

Distributed by NATIONAL BOOK NETWORK

Photos by Jim Meuninck unless otherwise noted

Maps by Melissa Baker and The Rowman & Littlefield Publishing Group, Inc.

British Library Cataloguing-in-Publication Information available

Library of Congress Cataloging-in-Publication Data
Names: Meuninck, Jim, 1942– author.
Title: Basic illustrated edible wild plants and useful herbs / Jim Meuninck.
Other titles: Edible wild plants and useful herbs | Falcon guide.
Description: Third edition. | Essex, Connecticut : FalconGuides, [2023] | Series: A Falcon guide | Includes bibliographical references and index. | Summary: "Discover how to identify and gather more than 100 of the most nutritious wild plants and useful herbs in the contiguous United States, prepare delicious recipes using your wild harvest, determine the identity of poisonous plants and poisonous look-alikes, and take charge of your personal health by making wild plants and herbs a part of your diet"— Provided by publisher.
Identifiers: LCCN 2022039780 (print) | LCCN 2022039781 (ebook) | ISBN 9781493068128 (paperback) | ISBN 9781493068135 (epub)
Subjects: LCSH: Wild plants, Edible—North America. | Wild foods—North America. | Cooking (Wild foods). | Illustrated works. | Field guides.
Classification: LCC QK98.5.N57 M48 2023 (print) | LCC QK98.5.N57 (ebook) | DDC 581.6/320973 —dc23/eng/20220825
LC record available at https://lccn.loc.gov/2022039780
LC ebook record available at https://lccn.loc.gov/2022039781

♾️™ The paper used in this publication meets the minimum requirements of American National Standard for Information Sciences—Permanence of Paper for Printed Library Materials, ANSI/NISO Z39.48-1992.

This book is a work of reference. Readers should always consult an expert before using any foraged item. The author, editors, and publisher of this work have checked with sources believed to be reliable in their efforts to confirm the accuracy and completeness of the information presented herein and that the information is in accordance with the standard practices accepted at the time of publication. However, neither the author, editors, and publisher nor any other party involved in the creation and publication of this work warrant that the information is in every respect accurate and complete, and they are not responsible for errors or omissions or for any consequences from the application of the information in this book. In light of ongoing research and changes in clinical experience and in governmental regulations, readers are encouraged to confirm the information contained herein with additional sources. This book does not purport to be a complete presentation of all plants, and the genera, species, and cultivars discussed or pictured herein are but a small fraction of the plants found in the wild, in an urban or suburban landscape, or in a home. Given the global movement of plants, we would expect continual introduction of species having toxic properties to the regions discussed in this book. We have made every attempt to be botanically accurate, but regional variations in plant names, growing conditions, and availability may affect the accuracy of the information provided. To positively identify an edible plant, examine a freshly collected part of the plant containing leaves and flowers, then present it to a knowledgeable botanist or horticulturist. Poison Control Centers generally have relationships with the botanical community should the need for plant identification arise. We have attempted to provide accurate descriptions of plants, but there is no substitute for direct interaction with a trained botanist or horticulturist for plant identification. **In cases of exposure or ingestion, contact a Poison Control Center (800-222-1222), a medical toxicologist, another appropriate health-care provider, or an appropriate reference resource.**

Contents

Acknowledgments

Feeling fortunate to have found this planet, I cherish it as my home and promise to keep it clean, tread lightly on its floor, and thank it daily for all blessings bestowed. I beg it to forgive my mistakes and ill manners. And when each of my given days is complete, I promise to sit quietly and listen to the earth sing, feel the air move, and revere all the green glory that is only found here.

But plants don't write, edit, lay out, and produce books. That job went to Meredith Dias, Paulette Baker, Melissa Evarts, and the entire staff at FalconGuides. Thanks! Without your help, the plants described herein would not get their due. And thanks to David Legere, who guided the project from germination to completion. Your kind, patient, and trusting approach coaxed these words from me, and your insightful and imaginative creation forged them into a desirable and helpful tool for aspiring foragers. Thank you!

I would be remiss if I didn't thank my spouse, Jill, and daughter, Rebecca, who have traveled side by side with me for more than 40 years.

Introduction

We eat plants or eat animals that eat plants; therefore our skin and bones, organs, blood and muscle come from plants. They are our food and medicine. In addition, they provide all the natural beauty, ambience, and culinary delights of a good life. They are the stuff of gardens and arboretums, forests and prairies, and mountain trails. Personally, they have given this average, ordinary man a lifetime of entertainment—simple pleasures, all free and described in the pages that follow.

Read thoroughly the "Foraging Rules" listed below. Follow these instructions and memorize the poisonous plants listed in appendix A. Although this information does not guarantee immunity from allergic reactions, it does provide essential protection against potentially toxic mistakes. The "Forager's Thirteen" chapter presents my favorite wild plant foods, most of which can be found from coast to coast. "Edible Mushrooms" is a novel chapter, an introduction to fourteen easy-to-identify mushrooms that will add hours of pleasure while hiking and numerous culinary delights for your table. The "Survival Foods" chapter presents plants from deserts, desert plants, lichens, ferns and grasses, and other extreme environments that provide a potentially lifesaving calorie margin. "Yards, Gardens, Prairies, and Meadows" is a collection of edible weeds and edible wildflowers found coast-to-coast in these environments—many of the best edibles come from this group. "Fruit and Berries," the next chapter, is a one-stop collection of fruiting vines, shrubs, and trees. If it's a fruit or berry you are looking at, go here. The "Wetlands" chapter covers edible plants found along streams and rivers, lakes and ponds. "Edible Plants of Eastern Forested Areas" provides a clutch of flowering plants found typically in hardwood forests. "Trees and Nuts" is a coast-to-coast look at shrubs and trees that produce nuts. "Edible Plants of the Mountain West" specifies plants found in the national parks and wilderness sanctuaries of Wyoming, Montana, Idaho, Utah, Oregon, and Washington. "Edible Plants of the Desert" describes food from arid environments. And "Marine Vegetables" provides pictures and insights specific to edible marine and tidal area wild plant foods.

Read this book from cover to cover. Use it in the field and at home. Cross-check different chapters, as there are close relatives of several plants found in different environments. Start with the "Forager's Thirteen," identify these plants and then progress to "Yards, Gardens, Prairies, and Meadows," which covers numerous familiar plants. As you forage through different environments, match the environment to its corresponding chapter and build your repertoire of wild foods.

Carry this book next to your heart or on your hip when seeking edible wild treasures to grace your table and serve to your friends. Many recipes are described here to excite you, but your unique personal discoveries will soon humble what I know. So think freely, my friend; invent and conceive—pass through this door of infinite possibilities and let your creative energy run wild.

WILD PLANT FORAGING RULES

1. It's a good idea to watch a plant through its growth cycle before eating it. This is helpful because many wild plants taste best just as they break through the ground, when they are small, furled, and difficult to identify. By watching them grow for a year, you will know what you are looking for in every season and where to find it.

2. Before eating any wild plants, study with an expert or take the plant to an expert for positive identification. Always cross-reference with two or more field guides. Make certain you have seen color photos of the plants; black-and-white photos or illustrations are not sufficient for positive identification.

3. After positive identification of an edible plant, taste only a very small amount of it. This precaution protects you from an allergic reaction or ill effects caused by misidentification. It also identifies the flavor and helps you imagine how to serve it.

4. Beware of the carrot family: Hemlock, water hemlock, and other members of this family are poisonous. Learn to distinguish hemlock and water hemlock from elder (elderberries) and wild carrot.

5. Practice conservation. Never collect more plants than you intend to use. Do not pick rare or endangered species. Work to restore wild plants from areas where they have disappeared. Join others in forays to remove invasive species—check with your state's cooperative extension services for details.

6. Avoid harvesting plants from polluted ground. Plants growing along roads may be tainted with benzene, lead, oil, and other auto pollutants. Wild plants dwelling near polluted streams and along cultivated fields may be poisoned with herbicides and pesticides. Forage carefully. Droppings from wild game and domestic animals may spread bacteria, viruses, worms, giardia, amoebas, and other forms of contamination into water that nurtures edible wild plants. Wash and cook all plants foraged from wetlands.

7. Purchase wild plants from seed and live-plant distributors (see appendix C: "References and Resources"). Grow them in your garden, close to your kitchen, and make wild foods an integral part of your diet.

Forager's Thirteen

Just outside the door, in the neighborhood, and in fields and forests dwell the Forager's Thirteen—edible wild plants that are free and provide superior nutrition. They possess a variety of delicious and satisfying flavors. These thirteen plants, growing from coast to coast, are easy to find, easy to prepare, and versatile. Put them in your garden and close to the kitchen for a robust and healthy diet.

1. **STINGING NETTLE** is number one. Transfer several of these plants to your secret garden and reap immediate rewards. Simply pinch off the top whorl of leaves from each plant, wash them, then steam or sauté the leaves for about 2 minutes to vaporize the stinging chemistry. Use the blanched leaves as a pizza topping, in stews and soups, and on sandwiches. Add it to your favorite sauces. Stuff it inside a sausage. Stinging nettle is versatile and provides a distinctive flavor you will come back for again and again. Here's the bonus: When you pinch off that whorl of leaves, the plant bifurcates and doubles your harvest the next time around. Add this tasty, mineral-rich plant to your diet today.

2. **WILD LEEKS** come in numerous varieties: wild chives, wild garlic, wild leeks, and wild onions. My favorite is *Allium tricoccum*, the wild leek, or what mountain folks call ramps. Find leeks in shady areas, typically forests east of the Missouri River. Simplicity is best when preparing this plant. All of it is edible. Sauté in olive oil with a few drops of soy. Cook until tender; eat leaves and bulb. By June the aerial parts of the plant die off and a flower spike with white florets leads you to the colony. Dig the bulbs and stuff them in olives: Purchase "party stuffer olives," reheat the brine, stuff a leek in each olive, return to hot brine, and seal the jar. When leeks are not available, stuff olives with other varieties of the wild onion family. Use the olives anywhere and everywhere: salads, martinis, pasta, sauces, sandwiches—you get the idea. More about this edible family later in the book. (More: p. 83.)

3. **VIOLETS** (*Viola* spp.), found coast-to-coast in various hues, are great in any dish where color and taste are prerequisites. Leaves and flowers are edible. Transfer them to your garden and let them compete with your pansies and tulip petals for space on the salad. (More: p. 88.)

4. **WATERCRESS** is a pungent spicy green that adds zest and character to any dish. Cream it into soup, stuff it in a frittata, pump up an omelet, or put zip in a salad. Find a spring or free-flowing stream near you, prowl around, and reward your effort with this spicy, high-kicking, versatile food. (More: p. 77.)

5. **CATTAILS,** found near your watercress and leek sources, have everything you need to survive—better yet, thrive. In June the flower heads are edible. Gather the male head, strip away the reproductive parts in quantity, and freeze. Use periodically to boost nutrition in pancakes, muffins, bread, pizzas, and all those other dishes and treats that require dough or batter. Steam the female heads like corn, add butter, and eat on the stick. Cattail roots and shoots are starch-rich, quick-energy food—best harvested in the fall or spring. (More: p. 69.)

6. **DAYLILIES** are found coast-to-coast. Harvested for their flower petals, they impart a mild onion flavor to the palate. Use in salads or stir-fries. Harvest just the petals, however, and discard the reproductive parts, which are bitter. The young shoots in spring are just OK, but give them a try—invent a surprising recipe. (More: p. 32.)

7. **SUNFLOWERS** have edible seeds, and the flower petals, although tough, can be chopped into sauces, soups, eggs, and more. Jerusalem artichokes, the premier sunflower foodstuff, provide young, edible shoots in spring, and the tubers of fall and spring are excellent. Cook tubers like potatoes, in every imaginable way. Sliced tubers make a starchy, flavorful base for a tortilla *española*. Yes! Go native, and use all these plants in your Mexican dishes.

8. **YELLOW WOOD SORREL,** often found in the yard or garden, is a lemony-tasting leprechaun. Eat both the small cloverlike leaves and flowers. Best in salads to balance the flavor of bitter greens and fun to nibble while watering the garden or hiking the fields. (More: p. 44.)

9. **PURSLANE,** famous as a rich source of omega-3 fatty acids, volunteers in most gardens. Don't have any? Then mix in a bag of store-bought manure and stand back: Invariably manure holds the seeds that will pay off. Add purslane to salads; cook in soups, sauces, stews; and eat it raw to get nutritional benefits. (More: p. 40.)

10. **DANDELION,** for many, is a noxious weed. OK, perhaps. But for me, it helps in salads when an appetite-stimulating bitterness is required. Tear the leaves from the petiole (midrib vein) and add pieces judiciously to salads and cooked greens. Add flower petals to any salad where you want yellow to entice the imbibers. (More: p. 31.)

11. CHICKWEED likes to compete with weeds wrestling for room along the edges of my lawn and neglected areas in the garden. A meaty "green"-tasting herb with an edible flower bonus, it's available, ready, willing, and able—free nutrition, three or four steps from the kitchen, a crunchy and tasty addition to the garden greens. (More: p. 28.)

12. BEEBALM provides two edible flowers with contrasting flavors: *Monarda fistulosa* and *M. didyma*. *Fistulosa* has a strong oregano flavor and is a pleasant addition to tea, refreshing in Italian sauces, and adds a delicate bite to Champagne. *M. fistulosa*'s red-flowered sister, *M. didyma*, has florets that taste like pineapple nectar; use accordingly—on salads; to scent and flavor white wines. Also try it on cold soups and ice cream.

Beebalm, red *didyma*

Beebalm, blue *fistulosa*

13. AUTUMN OLIVE is an invasive shrub with juicy and sweet edible drupes, fleshy skin-covered fruits with a single central seed. The drupes are available in September. The fruits are abundant—a roadside treat, often found in large numbers along roadsides and fencerows. Eat it on the run, but be careful not to bite the hard seed and chip a tooth. Abundant east of the Mississippi, in the Prairie

states, in northern wetter regions of the West, and in the Pacific Northwest. (More p. 45.)

Edible Mushrooms

Mushroom foraging, like foraging for edible wild plants, is rewarding. But few try it because of inadequate knowledge and a lack of experience fueled by fear. Here are fourteen mushrooms that are relatively easy to identify and safe to eat. These mushrooms offer variety and are available at different times throughout the year. The list is organized by ease of identification, availability, and season.

CAUTION: Like wild plants, there are dangerous mushrooms. I recommend you have at least four field guides (I have six) and key out any new or unknown mushroom in all four. Then make a spore print by placing the mushroom cap on a piece of black or white paper to ascertain the spores' color and shape. Make certain all the characteristics of the mushroom match what you have read and discovered in the field. For first experiences, always forage with a knowledgeable and experienced expert. Botanical gardens, state parks, and universities may offer mycology (study of fungi) field trips. My three books in the resources section have stringent guidelines—read them. Never eat a mushroom until it has been positively identified.

NINE MUSHROOM-GATHERING STRATEGIES

To identify a mushroom, follow this advice:

1. Use *four or five* field guides (the more the better) to cross-reference each find. Hunt with a mycologist or expert.

2. Discover and understand basic mushroom structure, the parts and elements that make a fungus a mushroom.

3. Develop field experience—the ability to recognize mushrooms and their habitats.

4. Discover their prey and partners—the biomes, trees, plants, and animals that mushrooms companion with, parasitize, or decompose.

5. Make a spore print and know how to read it, which may require a microscope.

6. Use chemical tests when necessary to help identify the mushroom.

7. Forage familiar ground.

8. Join a mushroom group or society.

9. Forage with a partner; you will find more mushrooms and have the luxury of a second pair of eyes for identification. I am color-blind. Whoa! Mushroom color and mushroom spore color are necessary to correctly identify a mushroom, so I don't go alone.

There are excellent mushroom websites for cross-referencing. Also read Jim Meuninck's detailed field guides: *Basic Illustrated Edible and Medicinal Mushrooms, Foraging Mushrooms Washington,* and *Foraging Mushrooms Oregon.*

With experience, the following mushrooms are easier to identify than most others.

MORELS

Yellow Morel
Morchellaceae *(Morchella americana, M. angusticeps)*

Identification: The yellow variety typically starts out gray and matures to yellow. Larger than black morels, it has a full body of pits and ridges of different shapes and sizes; yellows appear a week or two later than blacks. They can exceed 10" in height but are typically in the 3"–6" range.

Yellow morel

Habitat: Gray (yellow) and black morels are often found about halfway down a slope in the woods, where spores have been washed and collected, usually in a tangle of brush. Dead ash, elm, apple, pear, and tulip trees are good places to look. West of the prairie region to the West Coast, find morels in burnouts, along the sides of trails, and along the edges of campgrounds. Use your food dehydrator to preserve these mushrooms if you are fortunate enough to get more than you can eat right away.

Food uses: Morels can be dried and stored, pickled, or simply rinsed and frozen whole. They are delicious in all dishes where mushrooms improve the taste: omelets, frittatas, pizza, pasta, burgers, veggie burgers (sauté with wild stinging nettle, asparagus, and red bell pepper). Sauté the first bunch of the season in a pinch of butter and olive oil: Dust with flour, then sauté.

Black Morel
Morchellaceae *(Morchella elata)*

Identification: These have a brain-like outer appearance, ridged and pitted, with pits arranged in columns; hollow in the middle; a conical cap that tapers; 2"–6" in height.

Habitat: Moist woods, under and around dead elms, hillsides under snags of dead logs, edges of trenches and runoff areas, fencerows of north-facing woods, burnout areas in the West. April and May in Michigan, later in the West.

Food Uses: Use in the same way you would yellow morels.

Black morels harvested in Oregon

Half-Free Cap Morel
Morchellaceae *(Morchella semilibera)*

Identification: Half-free cap morels are small, 1"–1½" wide; proportionally the stem is long, up to 6". Half-caps have brownish ridges and conical caps. Pits are nearly parallel, deeply pitted yellow brown within. The bottom half of the cap is free from the stem, the lower half of the conical cap hangs like a skirt; both the cap and stem are hollow.

A handful of half-free caps

Cut the mushroom in half lengthwise and you will see the skirt attachment that is indicative of this species.

Habitat: Found on the fringes of coniferous forests and areas of birch and mixed hardwoods; moist shady to partial shade areas. A half-free cap that is similar but a different species is located west of the Rockies. Half-free caps are found a few days before yellow and black morels.

Food uses: Edible; prepare as you would other edible morels.

CAUTION: There are several morel look-alikes; next is one. Like all mushrooms, cook before eating them.

False Morels
Discinaceae *(Gyromitra* spp.)
Morchellaceae *(Verpa* spp.)

False morels are included here as a potentially toxic look-alike. I avoid these mushrooms. False morels *(Gyromitra* spp. and *Verpa* spp.) look similar to the edible morels but are strangely folded, as if nuked with radiation. They do not express the open hollow body of edible morels. There is

Folded and convoluted *Gyromitra*

tissue inside the semi-hollow spaces as seen when sliced longitudinally.

Habitat: Found in the same places as edible morels at the same time or even earlier.

DRYAD'S SADDLE

Polyporaceae *(Polyporus squamosus)*
I turn to this mushroom when morels are unavailable. Dryad's saddle is abundant, easy to identify, and available all year long. The flavor is not great, but it's good enough when thoroughly cooked and immersed in a soup or stew.

Identification: Forming shelves, this mushroom, often found in large clusters, is fan shaped, up to 15" in diameter, and pale tan to creamy yellow in color, with brown scales. This is a pored mushroom with a tough stipe. Flesh is white, more tender near margins.

Habitat: Prefers wet woods and is best picked after a substantial rain (most tender then). Found in marshes; along streams; on dead timber, stumps, and dying trees of all kinds.

Dryad's saddle

Food uses: Pick fresh young specimens that are wet and soft to the touch. A fresh *P. squamosus* releases a watermelon-like odor when torn. The mushroom gets tougher as you move toward the stem; use the tender outer edges. Eat both fresh and cooked.

PUFFBALLS

Agaricaceae *(Calvatia gigantea, Lycoperdon perlatum)*

Identification: Puffballs range from small to large (1"–12" in diameter), whitish to brown (but not green, red, orange, or pink), oval to round or pear shaped; edible when fresh. Larger ones are easier to identify. They grow flat on top of the ground, without a distinctive stem. Be certain to slice the mushroom in half to check for gills or what may be the development of a gilled mushroom—a possible toxic amanita. Amanita gilled embryos emerge as adults from egg-shaped capsules; these capsules resemble a small puffball, but puffballs when sliced open do not present gills.

Eastern puffball

Habitat: Found on open ground under trees and shrubs and often in lawns. In Michigan we start seeing *Calvatia*

Spiny puffball *(L. perlatum)* found in Montana

gigantea in late August and September. Our favorite little brown puffball, found on dead maple and beech, appears at the same time. The small western variety, typically available in July (Montana), is found on open ground under pine trees and shrubs, often in lawns. *Lycoperdon perlatum* is found along forest roadsides and in driveways under pines from summer through fall.

Toxic *Scleroderma*

Note: Find puffballs of various species from coast to coast. Larger ones are easier to identify. Pick, cut open, and make certain the inside is white and not yellowing—and that there are no gills.

Food uses: I slice large puffballs thinly and dry them in a food dehydrator. Powder the end product and stir into cooked dishes (1 tablespoon to 1 quart broth) when you want to impart a mushroom flavor. Fresh mushrooms are breaded and sautéed or deep-fried. The flavor is good; the texture is mushy.

> **CAUTION: Scleroderma citrinum *is a toxic puffball look-alike with distinctive interior. Always break open a puffball to see if it is a potentially harmful* Scleroderma *or full of spores and thus not good to eat.***

OYSTER MUSHROOMS
Tricholomataceae *(Pleurotus ostreatus, P. pulmonarius)*
Oysters were abundant and free for the picking yesterday, Sunday, May 2, the earliest date we have ever found them. I found them on dead beech, poplar, ash, and maple. They will be available through December.

Oyster mushroom (*P. pulmonarius*)

Identification: Oysters typically grow in large colonies and are gilled. Gills (lamellae) are the thin radiating blades beneath the cap of the mushroom, and with the oyster species the gills are attached and run down the stem. Stem (stipe) is off to the side, supporting a funnel-like cap. *P. ostreatus* (a fall mushroom, October and occasionally throughout the winter) starts out white and ages to slate gray, then light brown. White to pale lilac–colored spores variable to lilac

Oyster mushrooms (*P. ostreatus*)

gray. *P. pulmonarius* is a white aging to gray mushroom found in late spring and throughout the summer. Prevalent on dead beech trees in the Midwest, and often abundant.

Habitat: Oyster mushrooms can be found on beech, maple, elm, oak, and birch. They grow in dense clusters—I once took a bushel off one downed beech. They will continue producing on the same tree or stump for several years, decomposing it; once the bark is gone, they find a new tree.

Food uses: I prefer the taste of oyster mushrooms over morels. Panfry them coated in panko (Japanese bread crumbs). They're also great by themselves or with your favorite red or white oyster cocktail sauce. They can be used as a pizza topping, as well as in eggs, sauces, and Chinese and Mexican dishes.

KING BOLETE
Boletaceae (*Boletus edulis*)
Boletes are putrescent and break down into a slimy, mushy, odorous mass after sitting too long unrefrigerated. They carry a good deal of water, so don't wash them before cooking—dry-brush; do not bathe.

Cep, or king bolete

Identification: 3"–10" in diameter, a bun-shaped mushroom with a moist, smooth, and viscous surface (like a browned hamburger bun). Color variable from biscuit brown, margins paler. Flesh is thick, often infested with worms, insects, and larvae. They have tubes instead of gills, with the tube ends appearing to be stuffed with pith, first white in color and turning yellow, olive, to olive-yellow as they age—solitary and scattered and occasionally in groups of 2 or 3.

> ***WARNING: Avoid boletes with red or orange pores (tubes) and ones where cap surfaces or pores turn blue when bruised, as these may contain a muscarine toxin. Avoid orange- and red-capped bolete look-alikes. Also avoid boletes with yellow pore surfaces that turn blue when bruised. Avoid orange-capped boletes altogether.***

Habitat: I find king boletes in and around Yellowstone National Park in late July, typically in recovering burn areas, with 3"–10" spruce and new pine growth and dead timber on the ground. Farther west, in Montana, I stumble over them in campgrounds and along the edges of streams around the first and second weeks of August. I found several in one day during a warm year on Glacier Creek Trail in the Swan Valley, near Condon, Montana.

Food uses: The mushroom is watery; slice it thin and sauté. I cook them crisp. Cook into dishes and then freeze. It is too moist to dry. Eat and prepare as soon as possible, as its shelf life is short.

CHICKEN MUSHROOM

Polyporaceae *(Laetiporus sulphureus)*
Find one of these large spreading shelf-like (bracket) mushrooms and you'll have food for days, if not weeks. Often found in vacant woodlots and near populated areas. No need to hike into the wilderness for this mushroom—it's easily seen from the road, often along roadsides clinging to trees.

Chicken mushroom found in Oregon

Identification: A lemon- to orange-yellow (darkening with age) bracket fungus, grows on trees; typically grows in a semicircle, taking the shape of a convoluted fan; has softly rounded edges; tubes are yellow, and when fresh a slight squeeze will exude yellow juice. Can spread across in fans over a dead log. I have seen them spread to 20' with slight breaks between growths, and I have seen them as small as 6" across. Smell is pungent.

Habitat: Grows on trees, typically oaks, but also willow, cherry, and yew—seasonally available from late spring until early fall. In Michigan they are available June–September.

Food uses: This is a chewy, juicy mushroom that requires cleaning. Pull apart segments (layers), brush, and wash (I use a hose). Blanching removes any bitter taste. Texture and flavor when cooked is like chicken. I sauté the mushroom to cook and remove moisture, then freeze and thaw later to use in stews, soups, pizza, and omelets. Ideal for vegetarians. Goes well in risotto and with curry and various homemade salsas.

HEN OF THE WOODS

Polyporaceae *(Grifola frondosa, Polyporus frondosus)*

Note: Jill, my wife, found a 35 pound hen of the woods mushroom in her secret place 2 years in a row.

Identification: Grows at the base of trees. Central section of branched stems terminates in individual caps. Grayish caps 1"–3" across, with wrinkled edges. Stems gray also; mushroom browns with age. Tubes instead of gills.

Hen of the woods found in Michigan

Habitat: Grows on trunks of dead and living trees and occasionally on stumps. Typically on oaks but also found on other deciduous trees. Found in late August–October in the northern tier of eastern states.

Food uses: Requires diligent cleaning, with many cracks and crevices containing dirt and an occasional creature; I use a hose. This tasty mushroom requires enough cooking to soften its tough texture (depending on freshness). It goes well in all mushroom dishes. It dries well for storage, but I like to cook it first and freeze it for later use.

WOOD EARS

Tremellales *(Auricularia auricula)*
I discovered these the first time while searching for morels—they were growing on small lengths of rotting wood. Found them throughout the summer; best after a soaking rain.

Wood ears

Identification: Rubbery fruiting body that resembles an ear; 1"–3" across. Has a jellylike texture and snaps in the mouth like cartilage. It is tan-brown with grayish hairs on the velvety inner surface. Stretch the mushroom to make certain it is elastic and rubbery. It produces white spores, and the surface, as mentioned, is rubbery.

Habitat: Woods, fringes of woods; grows on wood (extremely rotted wood)—wood that can be shredded with your fingers. Many sources mention elder trees as a preferred habitat. Although available for several months, I find it rarely, and often in unlikely mushroom habitats.

Food uses: Wash thoroughly, then add to Asian-style stir-fries, or simply sauté in butter. Interesting chewy texture and surprisingly good taste that holds up either dried or frozen in cooked dishes. Great in sauces. Cook with wild leeks, thicken with sour cream, and serve over toast.

HONEY MUSHROOM

Tricholomataceae *(Armillaria mellea)*
In late summer and early fall, honey mushrooms appear in large numbers around the base of trees, stumps, and occasionally in the lawn, living off a submerged root. This is a destructive parasitic fungus that destroys many trees before their time.

Honey mushrooms

Identification: Cap size ranges ¾"–8"; color varies from honey-like to dark brown, clearly visible yellow cottony ring; stem varies 2"–6" and is tough and fibrous (usually not eaten); gills vary from off-white to dark brown. Flesh is white with strong, sweet odor. Stem base is fused, and there is almost always a cluster of tiny scales at the cap's center. Found in large clumps, dispersing pale cream, smooth, elliptical spores—do a spore print to be certain this is the right mushroom. Choose carefully, identify with the help of an expert, as there are nasty look-alikes.

Habitat: Found in both deciduous and coniferous forests, on living or dead trees, stumps, and buried roots. Found from early summer to early winter and may reappear at the same location in consecutive years and occasionally in the same year.

Food uses: Boil caps for 2 minutes in lightly salted water, discard water, then use mushroom caps. Sauté, cook in sauces, thicken in cream seasoned with garlic and fresh basil. Cook in recipes and store in freezer. Drying toughens the mushroom, and it does not reconstitute easily.

LION'S MANE
Echinodontium *(Hericium erinaceus)*
This mushroom, always a surprise, is found inside a hollow log or hanging from a tree or stump. Various species are found in the western, eastern, and southern states.

Identification: 2"–20" across; a white, spiny mushroom that yellows with age. Dangling white teeth give this fungus its common name. Teeth may be up to

Close-up of lion's mane spines teeth

1½" long and give the fungus the appearance of a lion's mane. Spore print is white. Fungoid attached to tree with a thick and solid white base—available in late summer and throughout the fall.

Habitat: Found singly and occasionally in pairs on the same wound from a decidu ous tree (hardwood). You may have to climb to harvest. Mature and old-growth woods are productive.

Food uses: A delicious mushroom sautéed and eaten by itself or served hot in a vegetarian sandwich. Store prepared dishes in your freezer. Soften mushrooms by cooking, which also eliminates some of the water from these hydrated specimens. Goes well with lemony marinades.

Survival Foods

This section covers edible wild plants that may provide you with the nutritional lift to sustain life in a survival scenario. Although not all are delicious, you should know and taste these plants to gain the confidence to eat them if you ever experience the necessity. These survival foods are widely dispersed in areas where you might get lost.

CACTUS
Barrel Cactus
Cactaceae *(Ferocactus* spp.)

Identification: Barrel cacti (numerous species) are at first columnar and mature to round; they may reach 8' tall but are typically smaller. They are barrel shaped (roughly round) and found in southwestern desert areas.

Habitat: Southwestern deserts, Texas, New Mexico, Arizona, Sonoran Desert, and Baja California.

Ripening barrel cactus fruit

Food uses: Flowers and fruit edible, but poor flavor. Do not drink inner moisture— too alkaline.

Medicinal uses: A cut piece of the cactus with moist side of the tissue placed over a wound is a cleansing surfactant, drawing blood, serum, debris from the wound site and then sealing it.

CAUTION: Spines are infectious; avoid contact.

Elephant Cactus
Cactaceae *(Pachycereus pringlei)*

Identification: Elephant cacti, on the other hand, are columnar to 65' tall and similar in appearance to saguaro cactus (*Carnegiea gigantean*). All these cacti have ribbed bodies or stems to allow for expansion when storing water.

Habitat: Find cardon or elephant cactus in southern California deserts, Arizona, Nevada, the Sonoran Desert, and Baja California.

Food uses: Flowers, fruits, and seeds are edible, a few more desirable than

Elephant cactus

others. Inner tissue is succulent and provides hydration when you need it. Cardon or elephant cactus is sought as a fruit or edible flower. In a pinch, go to what is available. Elephant cactus seeds are ground and added to olive oil, seasoned, and used as a sauce (salsa).

Medicinal uses: Inner flesh of stems is surfactant (absorbing) and can be laid over open wounds.

Note: Discover more edible desert plants in the "Edible Plants of the Desert" chapter.

REINDEER LICHEN; REINDEER MOSS
Cladoniaceae *(Cladonia rangiferina)*

Reindeer lichen

Identification: Lichen fungus is light colored, grayish-white or brownish-gray. Arms are called thalli and are branched 1, 2, or 4 times. Main thalli are thickest and still very thin (1.5 mm, plus or minus). Thalli can form extensive mats up to 6" thick. To me it looks like an enlarged multi-dendrite nerve cell. Lichen lives in a symbiotic association with a photobiont (*Trebouxia irregularis*) that provides the necessary mechanism to photosynthesize food for the lichen.

Habitat: This cold-tolerant lichen is found in boreal pine forests of northern Michigan, Minnesota, and east along the northern half of the Appalachian Trail as well as the Mountain West and north through the tundra to Alaska. Grows on humus, soil over rock, and on rocks—plus the plant detritus that makes up tundra.

Toxic wolf lichen on Douglas fir, Mount Rainier

Food uses: Edible fungus, poor tasting, chewy; a survival food. Soak in water to reduce acid content and then chop into bouillon, grit your teeth, and sip—high in vitamins, minerals, and antioxidants. Experiment. If lost on the tundra or in alpine areas where the lichen is available, chewing on it may give you a lift and the energy to stay alive. Boiling softens it and reduces acid—drink as tea. Occasionally used to flavor Scandinavian grain or potato distilled alcohol liquor called aquavit; it is used in a similar manner in Russia.

CAUTION: Wolf lichen **(Letharia vulpina)** *is a toxic lichen containing the poison vulpinic acid. The lichen is found on trees, typically conifers of the West and Northwest, and is bright yellow-green.*

Medicinal uses: Northern native tribes use the lichen in decoctions and as food to remove kidney stones. Chemistry in the lichen is under study for its propensity to kill prions indicated in transmittable spongiform encephalopathies.

Note: The Déné people of the Arctic kill caribou bingeing on reindeer lichen for their meat and then extract the stomach to access the reindeer lichen being digested within. The lichen is mashed with the animal's blood. The combination is then set aside to ferment for 3–5 days and sometimes longer, depending on temperature, after which the fermented food is cooked and eaten. The lichen is slow growing (¹⁄₁₆" or less per year); it takes decades to restore tundra and other environments destroyed by human recreation and oil exploration.

FERNS AND THEIR FIDDLEHEADS

Fiddleheads, or croziers, are the tightly curled young fronds of ferns rising from the ground on a stem (the rachis shaft), the new growth that emerges in the early spring. Various species are found in all states and are available from March to June, depending on altitude and latitude. A few species of ferns also produce fiddleheads in the fall and late winter.

The entire fern is made up of several fronds; the area just above the ground and up to the base of the fern's blade is the stalk. Attached to the stalk and beginning where the blade forms and continuing to the top of the blade is the axis. It is the stem where pinnae (leaflets) of the fern form; each pinna is made up of smaller leaflike structures called pinnules. Spore-containing fruiting bodies of a fern are called sori.

> *CAUTION: All the ferns covered here have been eaten by foragers and indigenous people for long periods. The bracken fern has been eaten for 7,000 years but has also been linked to cancer when eaten multiple days as primary nutrition in laboratory animals and during field experiments. Drinking milk from fiddlehead-fed cows has been linked tangentially to cancer. There is evidence that bracken fern fiddleheads may cause cancer. The carcinogenic chemistry is concentrated in the furled head and not as much in the roots or the rachis (stem) below the head. You are in charge of your health; you make the decision. I would not hesitate to eat them in a survival situation and have done so—raw. Raw fiddleheads, however, can carry foodborne illness and parasites and may cause stomach upset if you eat too many of them. When gathering fiddleheads, never harvest all of them from a single emerging plant—that would destroy the entire fern. It is best to take just 1 or 2 coils from each plant. Note: Bracken fern is not listed in this guide because of its potentially dangerous nature.*

Ostrich Fern
Onocleaceae *(Matteuccia struthiopteris)*

Identification: Identify ostrich ferns by their smooth, green stem with a deep (wide), U-shaped groove on the inside of the stem. They grow in vase-shaped crowns, 6–8 fronds per crown; crowns may be covered with moss. The previous year's growth may be apparent (dark and dried). As the fronds emerge, they are

covered with a brown sheath. The
fiddleheads are never furry or hairy,
always smooth. Leaves grow to 5'–7'
tall and 12" wide with 20–50 pairs of
leaflets—leaflets smaller toward the tip
and toward the base. Fertile leaves are
in the center of the outer leaves. Fertile
leaves are smaller.

Habitat: Damp rich soil. Climate zones
3–7, with some sun. Found along forested streams and ponds. Transplant to
a damp partial-shade place for beauty and food.

Vase-shaped ostrich fern

Food uses: Fiddlehead (crozier) is edible. Prepare when tightly curled. Parboil, then
sauté with oil or butter.

Medicinal uses: Fiddleheads have been used as a gargle, eaten as a laxative, and
applied as a poultice over wounds and boils. No scientific evidence to support
these traditional uses.

Maidenhair Fern
Polypodiaceae *(Adiantum pedatum)*

Identification: Shiny black (or dark
brown) wiry stems supporting delicate
leaflets, 15–40 leaflets per leaf, roughly
providing the appearance of a fan.

Habitat: Several species found from
coast to coast in lowlands, coastal
areas, and mountain arenas; prefers
shade and moisture. Often found clinging to the rock walls of a waterfall on
the shady side.

Maidenhair fern

Food uses: Fiddleheads are edible. Pick when tightly coiled; after unfurling, the
fiddleheads and whole plant are inedible—a marginal food, for survival use only.
Fiddleheads are a gourmet food in Japan. Steam fiddleheads, then sauté in oil or
butter before eating.

Medicinal uses: Leaves of plant are styptic; apply to wound to stop bleeding. Leaf
tea used to rinse hair.

Cinnamon Fern
Osmundaceae *(Osmundastrum cinnamomeum)*

Identification: These familiar fiddleheads emerge from the base of the plant and
unfurl into the classic fern shape: large, erect, pinnately compound, yellow-green,
sterile fronds (2'–4' long, taller in very moist areas). The fronds remain attractive

throughout the summer and turn yellow in autumn. Separate spore-bearing, stiff, fertile fronds appear in early spring, quickly turning brown. **Tip:** Get personal help at your botanical garden when attempting to identify ferns. Once identified in the summer, make a mental note or take a photo of the location so you can find the fiddle-heads next spring.

Cinnamon fern

Habitat: Found in moist, shallow wetlands; boggy grounds; along streams, shaded bluffs with seepage or falling water spray. Range is from Minnesota south, including Texas; east to the coast, including Florida; and north to Hudson Bay.

Food uses: Cinnamon fiddleheads are edible. Follow cautionary cooking procedure: Boil and sauté.

Medicinal uses: Root decoction rubbed into arthritic joints for relief. Root is also chewed and a small amount swallowed, with the remainder directly applied to snakebites.

Note: This is the first species of fiddlehead I ever ate, in 1982. Memorable, and the memory is not good—a rather bitter-tasting fern. The plant's name refers to the cinnamon-colored fibers around the foot, or base, of the fern. Fiber from the roots of cinnamon fern is used to pot orchids.

Sword Fern
Dryopteridaceae *(Polystichum unitum)*

Identification: Grows to 6' tall from tight, spreading clumps. Pinnae (the small leaflets attached to the frond) alternate on the stalk. There is a small lobe or hilt at the base of each pinna; pinnae are similar to Christmas fern pinnae of the eastern United States.

Sword fern

Habitat: Shady low-altitude, moist areas of the northwestern states, including California to Alaska, and east to Idaho. Spotty in the Black Hills of South Dakota and California's Guadalupe Island.

Food uses: Edible fiddlehead and edible tubers attached to rhizome. Northwestern First People roasted the rhizomes, peeled them, and ate the food when salmon were not available and other food sources were in short supply. Hmm! Not so good, eh?

Medicinal uses: Poultice; warm, wet applications of chewed leaves are used by First People on sores, boils, and skin inflictions and irritations. Roots (rhizomes) in decoction used to control dandruff.

Sensitive Fern
Dryopteridaceae *(Onoclea sensibilis)*

Sensitive fern

Identification: Fiddleheads emerge in spring as dark red stems with short white hairs along main rib and veins. Brown scales present on emerging stems. Fern will grow 11"–30" tall with bright green leaves. Most noticeable feature is the flattened and obvious winged stem with widely spaced, smooth-edged leaflets. Stem becomes dark brown to black and is flattened and winged, especially the upper area of the stem. Straggling leaves expose the creeping rhizomes that can engender thick mats of roots and large colonies of the fern.

Habitat: Tolerates numerous biomes in partial shade, shade, and even sun. Look in moist woods, thickets, wet meadows, swamps, pond edges, and wet edges of lakes. Range is all the eastern and midwestern states, including the prairie states and parts of Wyoming, Colorado, and Montana. Rare in California and the Northwest. Not found in the Southwest except for Texas.

Food uses: The unfurled early fiddleheads are parboiled, sautéed, or fried and then added to prepared foods or soups and salads. As with all fiddleheads, eat sparingly; one or two side dishes every spring should be safe enough.

Medicinal uses: Anecdotal reports suggest a decoction of the plant prevents baldness and may alleviate pain following childbirth. Decoction of the root is said to improve fertility in women and to strengthen them after childbirth. Infusion of whole plant or decoction of the root applied to breast improves lactation. Root poultice applied over cuts and abrasions.

Note: One of the easiest ferns to identify because of its winged stem.

THE GRASSES

A few years ago I presented to the Wilderness Medical Society, a group of medical doctors and advanced degree scientists. The topic was the overlooked value of grass and grass seeds as a survival food. I suppose we have all picked a stem of grass, stuck it in our mouth, and sucked on its vital juices. That practice, under severe conditions where moisture and sugar are unavailable, may save your life. Grass fiber is not digestible, so spit out the cud.

> *CAUTION: Excessive and prolonged use of certain grasses may have a toxic effect. Arrow grass (Triglochin palustris) contains the cyanide compound prussic acid; rye grass (Paspalum dilatatum) may harbor ergot; fescue from the Poaceae family may harbor toxic fungus galls; Johnson grass (Sorghum halepense) contains prussic acid; and foxtail (Alopecurus pratensis) and other species have hard and sharp chaff covering the seeds. If not carefully winnowed, they can pierce the soft tissue of any animal, including humans and pets. Be careful and judicious when foraging. A good resource for learning more about grasses: Grasses: An Identification Guide by Lauren Brown.*

Medicinal uses: Grasses (green grasses) may be used for binding gauze and poultices over wounds.

Note: For more edible grasses in this book, see cattails, wild rice, reed, plantains, and other grasses and grasslike plants that are found in their environmental niche. Consider the grasses described next as survival foods.

Beach Grass
Gramineae *(Ammophila breviligulata)*

Identification: Grows to 3½". Produces a single long flower on a tall stem. Leaves are narrow, basal. Plant is stiff. Tall stiff flower is pale yellow and slightly purplish.

Habitat: Found on sand dunes bordering bodies of water worldwide. Flowers in July; seedless flower persists through the winter.

Beach grass, Oregon, Pacific coast

Food uses: The roots (rhizomes and stolons) of this plant are softer and often moist, but you will have to dig for them. Harvest seeds when available. Seeds of this grass and others may be ground into flour; a bit tedious, but give it a try. Beach grass seeds are edible and best harvested early.

Medicinal uses: Wound binding.

Note: This common grass knits together sand dunes along the Great Lakes and dunes near larger bodies of water, both large and small, in numerous places around the Earth. If you're ever shipwrecked, look for sand dunes; the grass is there.

Foxtail
Gramineae (*Alopecurus* spp.)

Identification: Grows to 3'. (Looks like timothy, described on next page.) The flower is shiny and soft to the touch; 1"–2" long, narrow cylinder.

Habitat: Fields, waste ground, damp ground, prairie edges, railroad rights-of-way, roadsides, vacant lots. Found April–October.

Foxtail: never shy and never too far away

Food uses: Chew on the stem, the soft and juiciest part near the base of the stem. Seeds edible and can be shaken into a handkerchief or plastic bag; add water and simmer until soft. The stems are fibrous. Once you have masticated all the juices, spit it out; it is not digestible.

Note: Wet grasses, including foxtail, can be put on meat that is cooking over hot stones to hold in the moisture and heat.

Medicinal uses: Binding wounds.

Sweetgrass
Poaceae *(Hierochloe odorata)*

Identification: A sweetly odorous perennial grass; grows in dense clusters. Flat leaves are smooth and undersides shiny, 5"–15" long. Leaves droop, as the stem is not rigid. Flower spikelets produce 3 flowers; lower florets with stamens are male, and the upper floret is dioecious, producing both sexes.

Sweetgrass, Kentucky

Habitat: Widely distributed in North America north of a line drawn from Virginia to northern California. Cultivated on Native American reservations. Establishes in the garden and is found along the edges of wetlands and streams, but will tolerate dryness. Hardy.

Food uses: Plant is used as a flavoring agent in various beverages, soft drinks, tobacco, and candy. The leaves of this plant are infused and imbibed—a tea. It is also used in flavoring vodka and gin.

Medicinal uses: Considered a mosquito repellent. This is a sacred herb for Native Americans and used in sweeping and smudging ceremonies, a cleansing plant to brush away evil spirits and open your heart so the good spirits can enter. A relaxing chew; spit out the pulp.

Timothy
Gramineae *(Phleum pratense)*

Identification: Perennial; 1'–3' tall. Narrow cylindrical flower is rough textured. Stem and flower are stiffer and not as shiny as foxtail. Flower at first is pale green and then tan.

Habitat: Common along roadsides and fields, sharing the same environments with foxtail except for wet areas.

Timothy, Montana

Food uses: Like foxtail, chew on the base of stem; extract moisture and spit out indigestible cellulose.

Medicinal Uses: Wound binding. In test tube and petri dish studies, sterile extracts of timothy arrested sarcoma 45 and a few other tumors.

Note: Valued grass for grazing animals.

Yards, Gardens, Prairies, and Meadows

AMARANTH
Amaranthaceae (*Amaranthus retroflexus, A. hypochondriacus*)

Identification: Sometimes referred to as redroot, *A. retroflexus* is a hairy, stout weed with ovate to lance-shaped leaves on long stalks; flowers in dense clusters on an elongated bristly stem. Seeds typically black. The plant flowers in July and August; seeds are available soon after. *A. hypochondriacus* is similar but has red-purple seed heads and produces more seeds per plant.

Green flowered *retroflexus*

Habitat: Roadsides, fields, and waste grounds east and west of the Mississippi River at lower elevations. *A. hypochondriacus* is a hybridized ornamental, and its seeds are a food source both in Mexico and Africa. In the United States its habitat is widespread and varied, having escaped ornamental cultivation. This species is drought tolerant and hardy and can be found in near desertlike conditions or on the edges of wetlands.

Amaranthus retroflexus

Food uses: Young shoots and leaves of *A. retroflexus* are eaten raw or cooked (see "Caution"). May be dried and reconstituted in hot water for winter food. Seeds used whole as cooked cereal or ground into flour and used to supplement flour for bread, muffins, etc. Seeds also added whole to bread, pancakes, and waffles. Pinole (atole) is a hot corn drink made with toasted amaranth seeds and roasted blue or white cornmeal. Spread cornmeal and amaranth seeds on a cookie sheet or aluminum foil. Toast in a 425°F oven 8–10 minutes. Add sugar and cinnamon, stir into hot milk, and simmer 15 minutes. Native Americans ate cooked leaves and seeds mixed with grease. Try a mixed-greens dish of young and tender amaranth leaves combined with mustard, plantain, dock, and nettle and cooked with bacon.

Amaranthus hypochondriacus

CAUTION: A. hypochondriacus leaves contain oxalic acid and have a high nitrogen content, especially when grown on high-nitrate soils. A concentration of nitrates in the human diet may cause stomach cancer and has been linked to "blue babies," a congenital defect of the heart in a newborn. A. retroflexus also concentrates nitrates. Either limit your diet to the seeds of these plants or eat the leaves sparingly.

Medicinal uses: Native Americans used this plant mixed with green corn in sacred rituals. Leaves are astringent and used to stem profuse menstruation.

ASIATIC DAYFLOWER
Commelinaceae *(Commelina communis)*

Asiatic dayflower, edible flowers and leaves

Identification: Common weed in many gardens. Erect stems collapse on themselves as they grow (up to 3'). Deep blue flowers, ½"–¾" wide, 2 rounded petals (like Mickey Mouse ears) with a small white petal behind the pair. Flower's ovary sheathed in 3 green sepals; 6 yellow-tipped stamens. Fleshy, oblong leaves, 3"–5" long, pointed tips. Leaves sheath stem.

Habitat: Found nationwide in gardens and on roadsides. Alien weed, originating in China.

Food uses: This free food comes up late every year. Young leaves and shoots can be added to salads. I get so many of these plants in my garden that I pull whole shoots, wash them, and add them to stir-fries. Entire flower is edible. As fruit matures, the seed capsule (tucked in the sepal sheath) is a crunchy treat. In late summer, flowers keep coming. You can eat seedpods for a healthful dose of essential oils and phytosterols.

Medicinal uses: In China, leaf tea is used as a sore-throat gargle and for urinary tract infections, acute intestinal enteritis, and dysentery. Tea is also used to reduce fevers, as a detoxicant, and as a diuretic to treat edema from joint swelling and pain from arthritis. Flowers contain isoflavones and phytosterols—cancer-fighting antioxidants. Seeds contain fatty acids and essential and nonessential amino acids.

ASTER, NEW ENGLAND, AND OTHER ASTERS
Asteraceae *(Symphyotrichum novae-angliae)*

Identification: Rose-purple daisylike flowers (a few varieties have white petals) that are ¾"–1¼" wide. Flowers have numerous yellow disk florets in the center and ray florets radiating out from the disk. Each plant supports as many as 75 flowers; plant is up to 50" tall. Arrow-shaped leaves clasp the stem. Stem is rough to the feel, with numerous branches. Leaves are numerous and have prominent venation prior to maturity. Lower leaves shed at flowering; leaves are toothless (glabrous).

Habitat: Species are widespread and numerous. Found in fields, along stream banks in wetlands, and on waste ground at various altitudes from coast to coast and north and south.

Food uses: Fresh and dried leaves and flowers are edible. Dried flowers may be added to dishes. Put fresh flowers in salads along with the leaves.

Medicinal uses: Steamed flowers inhaled for sinuses. Infusion of flowers and root (tea) used to treat ear infections. Tea also reported to relieve gas and related stomachaches. Tea may reduce fever. Native Americans used the plant to treat numerous illnesses: infusions for diarrhea, fever, earache, gas pain. The dried blossoms were also snuffed for similar purposes or the steam vapor inhaled. The flowers and roots were both used. Smudge (smoke) of plants use to revive unconscious patient.

Food for bees and us

Note: In late summer the plant is widespread in the wild and in gardens. All asters are essentially nontoxic. A few people may get dermatitis from handling; if so, wash hands after touching asters. Favorite plant for bees and butterflies.

BURDOCK
Compositae *(Arctium lappa)*

Identification: Biennial; first year's growth sprouts broad elephant ear–like leaves (heart-shaped) that grow directly from a deep taproot. Second-year leaves are slightly smaller; mature plant is many branched and spreads 7'–8', although often much smaller. Flowers are crimson with inward-curving bracts that eventually form the

Edible root of burdock

mature seed capsule, which is a burr. This is the plant that deposits burrs on your dog and your trousers. Break open the seed capsule, and plant the seeds.

Habitat: Found in the Northern Hemisphere, temperate zone, in gardens, along roadsides, and just about every place you walk your dog, providing an entertaining burr-pulling party. My favorite site is a lowland marsh with rich muck that produces outstanding specimens.

Food uses: Harvest roots in autumn or spring of the first year's growth. Root may be 20" or longer. Peel the root, wash, slice diagonally, and stir-fry, steam, or sauté. First year's leaves may be peeled, cooked, and eaten. Slivered roots taste great on pizza for texture and flavor. Cut and peel second-year flower spikes, then sauté or steam.

Medicinal uses: Historically used to treat immune system deficiency and skin conditions. Leaf infusion (tea) used for chronic skin problems. Root oil used the same way: Soak the chopped root in olive oil in the refrigerator for 1 month. Root as food considered antidiabetic, regulating blood sugar when lightly cooked. Root tea and eating the root reported to treat acne. Root polysaccharides said to lower blood sugar; polysaccharides require more steps in digestion, thus the release of glucose is slow and gradual. According to a Japanese study, the root is antimutagenic (anti-cancer) in animal studies.

WARNING: Avoid if pregnant or lactating.

Note: The root, called gobo in Asian markets, sells for as much as $8 a pound. It's free in your backyard, so put it there. Pull burrs off a dog or your trousers, crush burrs to release seeds, and spread seeds on scuffed soil in November. Plant thickly; thin seedlings in May.

CHICKWEED
Caryophyllaceae *(Stellaria media)*

Identification: Chickweed is an alien annual native to Europe. It is low and spreading, germinating in cool, wet weather. Leaves are opposite, smooth and elliptical in shape, up to ½" wide and 1" long. Flowers in shades of white, pink, purple, and red—typically white. This weed can produce seeds 5 weeks after germination and produce seeds for months, each plant producing over 800 seeds; the seeds can lay dormant in the soil for up to 10 years.

Chickweed

Habitat: Thrives in a variety of conditions but prefers moist, shady locations—yards, lots, streamsides, gardens.

Food uses: Add to salads and other foods. Mildly floral, grasslike flavor. It can be eaten raw or cooked as a vegetable. Flowers are edible; the whole plant can be chopped coarse and stir-fried with other vegetables.

Note: The edible flowers provide nectar for elfin butterflies, syrphid flies, and other beneficial insects.

Medicinal uses: Renowned diuretic. Used as a soothing poultice over insect bites and stings and claimed to be an effective fresh plant poultice on cuts, boils, abscesses.

CHICORY
Compositae *(Cichorium intybus)*

Identification: Biennial or perennial to 4'; stem is erect, with few branches. Lanceolate (lance-shaped) leaves in a basal whorl, as well as additional smaller upper leaves on stem. Blue flowers (rarely white or pink) with square-tipped rays; a dandelion-like root. Plant blooms July–September.

Habitat: Conspicuous flowers along roadsides, disturbed areas, fields, meadows, waste ground nationwide.

Food uses: The root can be dried, roasted, mixed with coffee beans, then ground to yield Cajun coffee. The flower petals are slightly bitter and add a nice contrast when stirred into cottage cheese (let the blossoms infuse the cheese overnight in the refrigerator). The slightly bitter flowers, like all edible bitter plants, are a healthful addition to salads, jump-starting the digestion process.

Chicory, roadside food

Medicinal uses: Root dried or fresh is decocted in water as a diuretic, dietetic, and laxative. Root tea stimulates digestion, improving peristalsis and absorption. Root decoction used externally to treat fever blisters. Cherokee used root infusion as a nervine—a tonic for the nerves. Homeopathic preparation used for gallbladder and liver complaints. Root decoction may reduce blood sugar. Root constituents are antibacterial in vitro. Animal studies show chicory extract slows heart rate.

> **WARNING: A few sources suggest long-term excessive use of chicory may impair vision. This has not been scientifically proven.**

CLOVER, RED
Fabaceae (Trifolium pratense)

Identification: Often 3 leaflets showing pale chevron on each leaflet. Flower head is round; petals are rose-purple.

Habitat: Common roadside companion throughout the United States.

Food uses: Petals can be batter-fried or eaten raw in salads. Whole aerial parts of plant can be infused to make a bland but healthful tea.

Clover, a cleansing tea

Medicinal uses: Tea from flowers Is flavonoid rich, providing antioxidant, anticancer protection. Skilled herbalists used this plant to treat cuts, burns, and liver ailments. Integral part of the ESSIAC anticancer formula consisting of burdock root, slippery elm bark, rhubarb root, watercress, sheep sorrel, blessed thistle, red clover, and kelp.

COMPASS PLANT
Asteraceae (Silphium laciniatum)

Identification: Tall prairie plant that can achieve 12' has deeply lobed (cleft) leaves. Large basal leaves 1'–2' long and half as wide. Hairy (fine white hair) leaves are smaller as they climb the plant; upper leaf tips are pointed. Flower-bearing center stalk is thick, stout, green to light green, and branches into several or numerous flower stems near the top of the plant. Yellow flowers (5–30 blossoms) are sunflower-like and 3"–4" wide. Seeds are ¼"–⅔" long with a black, papery husk over the nut meat; odor of seed is resinous. Resinous gum produced near top of the stem. Taproot may drive 15" deep.

Habitat: Prairies, roadsides, railroad edges. Visit your local restored prairie and you will find the plant. In the eastern, midwestern, and prairie states, they are found in restored prairies replanted over old community waste sites and in state university botanical gardens.

Food uses: Seeds are trail munch or may be added to cereals and baked goods; taste similar to sunflower seeds.

Compass plant in Iowa, October

Medicinal uses: An infusion of the leaves was used as an emetic and to treat asthma and coughs. Smaller roots attached to taproot were used in decoction as an emetic. Resin is encouraged to ooze with a slit of the stem using a knife; the resin is chewed as a breath cleanser or gum.

Note: Basal leaves are arranged in a north–south axis, thus the name compass plant—useful information should you get lost in a high-grass prairie; the leaves are a compass. Once the plant is seen, it is always remembered. Seeds edible in October. I have been eating the seeds for years. There is little documentation in the literature, but I am still vertical and walking 80 years into a wonderful journey. Put the black seed in your mouth, tease out the nut from the husk, and chew.

> *CAUTION: An unnamed anti-neurotoxin has been studied in the plant. The word **toxin** is used often in the literature as a caveat to those who would use the plant. Further research on my part suggests that the plant's anti-neurotoxin property is a good thing, but more research is needed.*

DAME'S ROCKET
Brassicaceae *(Hesperis matronalis)*

Identification: Dame's rocket is a showy flowered biennial or short-lived perennial. It has 4-petaled flowers. Leaves are simple, lance-shaped, alternate with toothed margins, and somewhat hairy. Leaves are smaller as they ascend the stem.

Dame's rocket flowers and buds

Habitat: Found along roadsides nationwide, most prevalent in the eastern United States. Considered an alien—a gorgeous and edible one.

Food uses: Flower buds may be cooked with other vegetables. Flowers are used to garnish plates and are edible, faintly sweet. Young shoots may be steamed, stir-fried, or sautéed. A versatile plant that blooms throughout the spring and summer.

Medicinal uses: Traditionally used to induce sweating, to treat cough, or as a diuretic to induce urination. None of these uses have been scientifically proven.

DANDELION
Compositae *(Taraxacum officinale)*

Identification: Basal whorl of toothed leaves. Yellow flower with numerous rays. Torn leaf and/or flower stem will exude white-colored latex.

Habitat: Common yard bounty. Found in temperate regions worldwide.

Food uses: No waste—eat flower, root, leaves, and crown. A vitamin- and mineral-rich salad green. Tear it into small pieces for salad; mix with thyme, fennel, and nasturtiums, along with other salad ingredients. Thyme and fennel balance the bitterness of dandelions. Make a mineral-rich tea from the roots and leaves. Gently simmer chopped fresh roots for a stomach bitters. Cook fresh leaves early in season with olive oil, bacon, and lemon juice.

It's all edible.

As season progresses, leaves become bitter: Pour copious amount of water on the late-summer plants—the morning harvest will be sweeter. Even when bitter, leaves are a healthy addition to a stir-fry; try with tofu. Or cook in oyster oil with cayenne, garlic, and strips of beet sauteed with leeks, kale, and turnip greens.

Medicinal uses: Dried leaves and autumn roots are infused or decocted as a liver-cleansing tonic, aiding digestion and cleansing the blood. It is a diuretic, traditionally used to treat PMS, has a mild laxative effect, and may relieve inflammation and congestion of gallbladder and liver. Native Americans applied steamed leaves externally (poultice) for stomachaches. Eating green leaves is considered a tonic and blood purifier; root taken to increase lactation, as a mild laxative, and for dyspepsia. The bitter taste of dandelion is an appetite stimulant and may help treating anorexia. Because the bitter dandelion root decoction raises hydrochloric acid in the stomach, it improves calcium breakdown and absorption, increasing bile production and therefore lowering cholesterol (1 bile molecule requires 2 cholesterol molecules from the liver).

DAYLILY
Liliaceae *(Hemerocallis fulva)*

Identification: Yellow, tuberous roots; long, narrow, lancelike leaves; orange lily flower.

Habitat: Found along roadsides; transplant to clean soil away from auto pollution. Throughout the United States. Shade and sun tolerant; excellent garden transplant.

Food uses: Onion-tasting flowers are flavonoid rich. Tease apart daylily petals from the whole flower and toss with salad greens. Flowers (without pistils and stamens) and unopened buds can be stir-fried or batter-dipped and cooked tempura-style. Try the sautéed flowers wrapped in wontons and steamed. Or wrap raw buds and flowers in a wonton, steam wonton, dip in soy

Daylily

and mustard—delicious. Buds can also be steamed, boiled, or deep-fried and then served with butter or cheese sauce. Harvest firm root tubers; add raw to salads or cook like a potato.

Note: Eat just the flower petals, not the reproductive organs—the stamen, pistils, anthers, and filaments are bitter.

Medicinal uses: Daylily buds contain more protein and vitamin C than green beans and asparagus. Traditional people used the extract of the herb to treat cancer. There is evidence that extracts of daylily roots and crowns are pain relievers, a diuretic, and an antidote to arsenic poisoning. Daylily flowers are known to possess antioxidant properties and cyclooxygenase (COX) inhibitor; inhibition of COX can provide relief from the symptoms of inflammation and pain.

> ***WARNING: If uncertain the plant is a daylily, use flowers and buds only when in bloom. Early growth resembles poisonous iris shoots (see appendix A: "Poisonous Plants"); daylily's yellowish tubers are distinctive.***

EVENING PRIMROSE
Onagraceae *(Oenothera biennis)*

Identification: Biennial that grows to 3' or more with fleshy turnip-like root. First-year plant is a basal rosette of leaves; second year is erect plant, conspicuous in the fall with its large seed-filled fruit capsules. Oblong lance-shaped leaves, pointed and finely dentate. Fragrant bugle-shaped yellow flowers are 1" long and grow

Evening primrose

from the leaf axils; western varieties have white, yellow, or pink flowers. Flowers open in evening and have 4 petals, 4 sepals, and 8 stamens. Fruit is linear-oblong, 4-sided, downy, ½"–1" in length, producing seeds that are dark gray to black with sharp edges.

Habitat: Found in gardens, along roadsides, on waste ground, and in fields and prairies up, down, and across North America. More than 20 species inhabit the western states.

Food uses: The root is edible. (Biennial plant; first-year root best. The fall or early spring root of second year is edible, but second-year root becomes too bitter by summer.) New leaves of first or second year are edible in salads and stir-fries. The leaves are tough and need to be cooked. Seeds poured from seed capsule (seed capsule looks like small, dried okra pod). Immature seed capsules may be cooked like okra but don't taste like okra—nothing like okra; not worth the trouble. But evening primrose seeds are available on cross-country ski trips throughout the winter. I pour them from the capsule and eat out of hand.

Medicinal uses: Seed oil is used to treat essential fatty acid deficiency and to lower cholesterol. Cholesterol-lowering effect proved successful in a double-blind crossover study conducted in 1996. Native Americans used warm root poultice to treat piles. Roots chewed to increase strength and endurance. Whole plant bruised, soaked, and used as a poultice on bruises and sores. Seed extract said to dilate coronary arteries and clear arterial obstruction.

HEAL ALL; SELFHEAL
Lamiaceae *(Prunella vulgaris)*

Identification: Blue to violet bract of flowers clustered in a whorl at the end of the square stem. Stem, when young, is erect. Plants are typically 6"–10" in height. Leaves ovate to lance shaped, margins are dentate to entire (smooth) and opposite.

Habitat: Found on waste ground, lawns, fields, and margins of woods nationwide.

Heal all

Food uses: Sauté small leaves with stinging nettle and add to soups. Aerial parts made into an infusion with mint leaves and a twist of lime.

Medicinal uses: Documented use by the Chinese for more than 2,200 years, self-heal used for liver complaints and improving the function of the liver. The whole plant used in infusion to stimulate the liver and gallbladder and promote healing—considered alterative and capable of changing the course of a chronic disease.

HOPS
Cannabaceae *(Humulus lupulus)*

Identification: A perennial climbing vine with pencil-thick stems that do not turn woody. The plant climbs through shrubs. Leaves are opposite, 3–5 lobed, and serrated. Male flowers are small, inconspicuous, and yellowish-green. Female flowers have numerous florets, and a fruit cone grows from the flowers. Cone may be yellowish to gray, depending on whether it is fresh or dried. The scales of the cone contain the bitter substance called humulene used in beer and digestive teas.

Wild hops

Habitat: It has escaped from cultivation and is found in marshes, meadows, and the edges of woods. Cultivated stands can be seen in Washington State, east of Seattle in the Yakima Valley, and in Idaho along the Canadian border.

Food uses: The fruit cone (gray to yellow), used in the production of beer, gives it a bitter flavor. The more hops, the greater the bitterness, as in Pilsner Urquell and popular IPA brews. Also used as a sedative tea. Cone-like flowers are placed in pillows to improve sleep. The young tender shoots of spring are edible; sauté.

WARNING: Contact with pollen has caused allergic reactions.

Medicinal uses: Infusion of the flower or seed cone is emollient, sedative, and a bitter digestive stimulant. Native Americans used it in sweat lodges by soaking leaves and throwing the flowers on hot rocks. Basque shepherds use the cones in infusion as a calming sedative and digestive. They drink the tea to settle jittered nerves and stimulate digestive juices to hasten peristalsis and catharsis. Pioneers and Native Americans also used the tea to treat fevers from acute infections. Research suggests that the flower tea may impart estrogenic effect. Although subsequent research has not shown this effect, it is a phytoestrogen.

Note: According to a few sources, smoking hops like marijuana (both plants contain the anti-inflammatory chemical humulene) may provide a mild sedative effect; the 2 species are related. To make a sleep aid, add about 1 teaspoon of dried flowers to a 6-ounce cup of hot water, just off the boil. Cover and let cool to lukewarm, then drink.

JERUSALEM ARTICHOKE; SUN CHOKE
Asteraceae *(Helianthus tuberosus)*

Identification: Yellow sunflower; broad ovate, rough leaves; lower leaves opposite, upper leaves alternate; hairy stem; tuberous root.

Habitat: Throughout the United States, along roadsides, gardens, fields.

Jerusalem artichoke

Delicious!

Food uses: Tuber peeled, sliced, and eaten raw; has taste similar to water chestnut. Also microwave, bake, or boil like a potato. This plant is worth looking for. I like it as a base for a tortilla *española* (frittata): Spread them on the bottom of an iron skillet, pour over 6 whipped eggs; add other wild plants (chopped), sharp cheese (grated); cook at 375°F for 15 minutes, serve (see recipe in appendix B).

Note: Add tubers to your garden and they'll provide a substantial food source that continues to reproduce year after year. Harvest tubers in fall and spring.

Medicinal uses: Tea made from flowers and leaves is a traditional treatment for arthritis. Inulin-rich tuber is slow to release sugars, making it a good food for diabetics.

LAMB'S-QUARTER; PIGWEED; GOOSEFOOT
Chenopodiaceae *(Chenopodium album)*

Identification: To 5' in height, with light green (grayish-green) leaves with pow-derlike substance beneath, coarsely toothed, with a goosefoot or diamond shape. Small green flowers in clusters, growing from top third of plant and many of the branches. Seeds are gray colored.

Habitat: Across the nation in meadows, along roadsides, in gardens, waste ground, edges of cultivated fields.

Food uses: Add lamb's-quarter leaves to salads, stir fries, and steamed wontons with quinoa, carrots, burdock root; roll wontons in quinoa seeds before steaming.

Lamb's-quarters

Hontzontles: Lamb's-quarters battered and fried

The herb flavors corn and fish dishes and Mexican foods. Seeds may be ground and used in baking recipes. Add seeds to pancakes and waffles, bread, pizza dough. Also great as a cooked cereal; best when part of a multigrain cereal. Cook it like rice.

Medicinal uses: Lamb's-quarter tea used for stomachache, scurvy, diarrhea. Also poultice over wounds and bites. In Mexico, cooked leaves and seed heads are believed to keep the digestive system clean and healthy. Cree used leaves for arthritis, rheumatism—washing joints and limbs with the decoction. Inuit people believe the leaves, when cooked with beans, dispel gas. Iroquois used a cold infusion of the plant to treat diarrhea. Leaves are high in vitamin C content (used to treat scurvy), and when eaten with seeds, the essential amino acid content is complete.

MILKWEED; COMMON MILKWEED
Asclepiadaceae (*Asclepias syriaca*)

Asclepias syriaca

Identification: Perennial to 4' with a single stem; leaves opposite, large, elliptical to 8" in length. Pink flowers in drooping clusters grow from leaf axils. Arabian slipper–like seedpod is striking.

Habitat: Edges of cornfields, waste ground, roadsides, railroad rights-of-way, meadows, dunelands, desert, gardens. Various species found nationwide.

Food uses: Native Americans prepared *A. syriaca* like asparagus before milky sap appears (cooked in 2 changes of water). Flower buds are prepared like cooked broccoli when harvested before they open. Flowers buds and seedpods are prepared as follows: Boil water, pour over seedpods, let water and pods steep for 5 minutes, then pour off water. Repeat: pour a second boil of water over once-steeped pods, pour off water, and then stir-fry in olive oil or butter. Many people use 3 water baths over pods—recommended for first encounters. Flowers may be dried and stored for winter use in soups, stews. Keep in mind that I have only eaten *A. syriaca*. Other species may be toxic. Do not experiment unless guided by an expert.

> **WARNING: Plant parts contain a cardiac glycoside that must be denatured by repetitive cooking. First-time users: Eat a very small bite of the plant to see if you have a reaction. Many people eat the plant, so it is contained here, but not without warning.**

Medicinal uses: Native Americans pounded or split the roots to expose their flesh for drying. Dried roots in decoction have a mild cardiac-stimulating effect—without the toxic effects of digitalis. *Be warned:* This should be practiced with medical supervision—*A. syriaca* contains toxic cardiac glycosides and requires careful preparation before use. Native Americans believed the plant was a lactagogue because of the milky white sap, per the Doctrine of Signatures, or "like treats like." Latex from leaves rubbed on warts and applied over insect stings and bites and spider envenomations. According to Duke and Foster in *Peterson Field Guide to Medicinal Plants and Herbs*, the plant is considered "dangerous and contraceptive"—respect this, and use the plant judiciously.

WARNING: Root decoction is emetic; may stimulate the heart. Some people may experience allergic reactions to the milky sap.

OYSTER PLANT
Asteraceae *(Tragopogon dubius)*

Identification: Looks like a large dandelion; grows 2'–4' tall, with a smooth stem and yellow flower head. Stem hollow just below flower head, yellow rayed flower, 2½" in diameter, blade-like leaves; entire plant may grow to 4', though typically less.

Oyster plant

Habitat: Dry areas, fields, open fringes of woods, fence lines, meadows, and burnouts. Found nationwide from east to west, north into Ontario and south to Texas.

Food uses: Young leaves boiled or sautéed. I have eaten flower petals, but do so judiciously, as I appear to be the only author who does.

Medicinal uses: Native Americans made a cold infusion of whole plant to treat animal bites and used latex sap as a milk substitute. Latex will dry and may be chewed; cathartic.

PLANTAIN
Plantaginaceae *(Plantago lanceolata, P. major)*

Identification: Several varieties are found across the United States. The difference is in the leaves: *P. major*'s leaves are broad and ovate; *P. lanceolata*'s leaves are narrow and lance shaped.

Plantain

Habitat: Discover these common plants on open ground, wasteland, edges of fields and roads, and lawns nationwide.

Food uses: In the spring I pluck whole leaves from my garden and yard, chop them into salads or sauté them with wild leeks, nettles, dandelions, and watercress. Cut summer and autumn leaves from the tough mid-leaf vein (rib) before adding to salads. Seeds added to baked goods improve fiber load.

Medicinal uses: Strip off flowering heads between thumb and forefinger into hot water to form mucilaginous drink for treating constipation. Crushed plant applied to dermatitis to treat poison ivy. Native Americans chewed the leaves, mixing in saliva and defensin (antibiotic in our mouths) to provide an antiseptic and immune-stimulating poultice to be applied to wounds, scrapes, cuts, and bruises. It is styptic, stopping blood flow. Tea is diuretic, decongestant, expectorant, and may be helpful in diarrhea, dysentery, irritable bowel syndrome, laryngitis, and urinary tract bleeding. Aucubin in plantain increases uric acid excretion by kidneys and may be helpful in treating gout. *P. lanceolata* extract from the fresh plant may fight colds (4 grams of herb to 1 cup boiling water), may alleviate symptoms of bronchitis and cough, and may reduce fever. It is German Commission E–approved for treating inflammation of the pharynx and mouth and for skin inflammations. Typically, a dose is 3–6 grams of the fresh whole herb (aerial parts when in bloom) added to 1 cup of water just off the boil. Let cool, then drink; take 3 or 4 times a day.

POKEWEED; POKE SALAD
Phytolaccaceae *(Phytolacca americana)*

Pokeweed

Identification: A smooth-skinned plant with purple stems when mature, to 10' tall but more typically 5'. Stems are hollow and usually marked with grooves. The root is long and thick. Leaves are ovate-lanceolate, alternate, 5"–10" in length, with entire margins. When rubbed, leaves provide a musty indicative scent. Flowers are on racemes, with a calyx but no corolla. Berries are purplish to black when ripe.

Habitat: From the Missouri River east to the coast and south to the Gulf. Found on waste ground, fields, roadsides, gardens.

Food uses: The young shoots of this plant are edible in the spring. Leaves are boiled in 2 changes of water. Avoid poke once the stem and leaf petioles have turned purple. The lectin content rises as the plant matures. Cooking destroys some of the lectins, and digestive juices get others. Your window of opportunity is short. This is an excellent-tasting green. If you are not certain, you can find these greens canned and commercially available.

Medicinal uses: Native Americans traditionally used the root poultice over rheumatoid joints. Berries made into tea for rheumatic conditions. Berry tea is also used to treat dysentery. Infusion of root used for eczema, ulcerated wounds, and to reduce swelling. Spread dried and powdered roots over cuts and sores. Plant used as a proven laxative and emetic. A leaf decoction mixed with other plants taken as a blood purifier and stimulant. Infusion of root and branches used in sweat lodges to produce steam, considered antirheumatic. Root pounded and mixed with grease and applied to bunions.

PRAIRIE DOCK
Asteraceae *(Silphium terebinthinaceum)*

Identification: Tall prairie plant rising from
a basal rosette of large spade-shaped leaves.
Leaves are thick and rough, especially underneath. They are large, from 19" long and 1'
wide. Older leaves turn dull and roughen. Petioles (leaf stems) are 5"–7" and are tough. These
leaves look like burdock or rhubarb leaves with
slender petioles. The tall flower stalk starts
from the ground in the center of the plant
and may shoot to 10' high. Stalk is green and
sometimes red, mostly hairless, and divides
into panicles of yellow daisy- or sunflower-like
flowers emerging from round, greenish buds.
Flowers 2"–3" wide with 15–30 rays striking
out from the numerous florets in the disk.
Blooms from late summer into the fall. Seeds
are flat and wind pollinated. Taproot can drive
itself 12' deep.

Prairie dock growing on a restored prairie

Habitat: Prairies in Michigan, Indiana,
Illinois, and most of the Midwest, west
to the mountain states, and south to
Georgia and Oklahoma. Occasionally
found along roadsides and railroad
rights-of-way.

Food uses: Seeds are edible—at least I
eat them. There is nothing in the literature about this, but I have been eating
them for years on prairie walks, pulling
apart the seeds from the mature flower

Prairie dock seeds

and squeezing out the seed meat from the black husk with my front teeth. They
taste like sunflower seeds, so bring along the salt.

Medicinal uses: The resin in the plant is a diuretic. Infusion is a general pick-me-up,
a tonic. Leaf tea is reported to be an emetic. Gum and resin from plant are used as
a cleansing dentifrice and/or chewing gum. These are all traditional uses, and the
products are not available over the counter.

Note: Numerous insects, insect larvae, and birds feed on the plant, including bees,
bee flies, grubs (cicada), beetle and wasp larvae, tumbling flower beetle larvae,
hummingbirds, and goldfinches—a veritable banquet for wildlife.

PURSLANE
Portulacaceae *(Portulaca oleracea)*

Purslane

Identification: Spreading succulent that sprawls through garden with thick, fleshy, shiny ovate leaves. Stems are many branched, supporting small inconspicuous flowers.

Habitat: Gardens and waste ground, even cracks in the sidewalk, from coast to coast. Volunteers sprout from com- posted manure.

Food uses: Purslane is a common garden plant, an alien creeper with ovate leaves, thick and succulent—eaten right off the ground, put in salads, and chopped into soup. The payoff is omega-3 essential fatty acids. Native Americans ate the leaves as a raw or cooked vegetable. It was also boiled in soups and with meats. Try it chopped in salads or in salad dressing, even turkey stuffing. Native Americans ate purslane raw with meat and green chiles, and it can be dried and reconstituted as a winter food. Cow manure (store bought) put on the garden invariably produces purslane.

Medicinal uses: Crush plant and apply as a poultice over burns and bruises or as a skin lotion. Juice used to treat earaches. Juice of whole plant considered a tonic. Used in the past as an antidote to unspecified herbal toxins. Infusion of leaf stems used to curtail diarrhea. Decoction of whole plant considered an antiseptic wash and was eaten as a traditional remedy to treat stomachache; also used to treat worms. Essential fatty acids may help prevent inflammatory conditions such as heart disease, diabetes, and arthritis.

SHAGGY SOLDIER; GALLANT SOLDIER
Asteraceae *(Galinsoga quadriradiata, G. alinsoga parviflora)*

Shaggy soldier for the pot and as a spice

Identification: Plant is 10"–16" tall, leaves about 1½" wide and 2½" long, toothed and hairy. Leaves are oppo- site, have pointed tips; older leaves just beneath flower become narrower, bases are rounded or tapering. Three leaf veins radiate palmately from base of leaf. The difference between the 2 species is primarily the hairiness, with *G. quadriradiata* more hirsute, and *G. parviflora* less hairy or glabrous (smooth). Leaf stalks are shorter as they get closer to the flower. Flowers are small, white, and about ¼" or less wide and rise from the leaf axils at the tips of branching stems; typically 5 white rays surrounding a yellow disk. Rays may number 4–8. Flower tips are notched 3 times. Seed is small and dry, slightly scaly.

Habitat: Gardens, cracks in sidewalks, fringes of disturbed ground anywhere they can get a foothold. Hardy through a few frosts. Available nationwide, more or less, depending on where you get your manure (see Note).

Food uses: Leaves, stems, and flowers are edible and, to my taste, very good. Eat leaves and flowers in salads raw; when the stems and leaf veins get tough, sauté or steam the plant. I drop older flowers and stems in soup (see appendix B for Guascas chicken soup). In Colombia and Peru *guascas* is the common name of these plants—aerial parts are a spice. The 2 plants are used interchangeably.

Medicinal uses: Gallant soldier contains ACE inhibitors and may lower blood pressure. In traditional medicine, both plants are crushed or juiced and applied to wounds and to relieve nettle stings.

*CAUTION: There is a similar-looking toxic Asteraceae, **Tridax procumbens**; the flower petals are similar but off-white. It is an invasive weed found in Florida (tropical and subtropical); according to the USDA it is, as of this writing, not found in other states.*

Note: I had been weeding this plant out of my garden for many years before I found that it was edible. It arrives as an alien in bags of manure purchased from my local Ace Hardware. In the bag are seeds of purslane and chickweed along with other desirables The seeds somehow (years ago) crossed the Mexican–US border (illegally) and are now welcomed as naturalized citizens.

SPIDERWORT; WIDOW'S TEARS; SPIDER PLANT
Commelinaceae *(Tradescantia virginiana, T. occidentalis, T. pinetorum)*

Identification: Leaves are long, tough, swordlike, smooth, with entire margins. Numerous leaves grow from the base (no stem). Flowers are orchidlike, in drooping terminal clusters, deep blue; open in the morning and closed by

Spiderwort

afternoon. The plant blooms continuously throughout summer. There are at least 4 species in North America.

Habitat: In my garden and along railroad rights-of-way, roadsides, fields, and prairies from coast to coast.

Food uses: Tender shoots of spring eaten raw or cooked. Flowers are edible throughout year; pick in morning before they wilt. Try them in salads, stir-fries, or right off the plant. Flowers dipped in egg white and coated with powdered sugar. Flowers are mucilaginous.

Medicinal uses: Root tea was used as a laxative and for female kidney disorders and stomach problems. Crushed and smashed aerial parts of plant used as a poultice over insect bites, stings, and to bind wounds. Aerial infusion also used to treat stomachache. Native Americans and pioneers used the crushed plant as a poultice to treat cancer. *T. occidentalis* tea used as a diuretic; infused plant said to be an aphrodisiac.

Mixteca tribe of Mexico bound Hernán Cortés's thigh wound with this plant, and it is credited for saving his life. As a garden perennial, this plant gives and gives and gives.

THISTLE, BULL
Onagraceae *(Cirsium vulgare)*

Identification: Thorny biennial; ¾" purple flower with numerous rays rises from spiny bract. Barbed, deeply cut leaves of the first year's growth eaten after the spines are stripped away with a knife—wear gloves when harvesting roots and leaves.

Bull thistle

Habitat: Coast-to-coast in northern-tier states, mountainsides, streamsides, waste ground, roadsides, dry and well-drained areas.

Food uses: Use a knife to strip thorny armor away from leaves. Eat raw or cooked; flavor similar to celery. Harvest leaves in the spring and fall. In summer, sprinkle flower petals over salads. Roots can be boiled, sliced, and stir-fried. Some folks steam the outer green bract around flower heads and eat it like an artichoke.

Medicinal uses: The Chinese use thistle teas and decoctions to treat appendicitis, internal bleeding, and inflammations.

WILD GARLIC
Liliaceae *(Allium sativum)*

Identification: Long, narrow, pencillike leaf stalk; flower head bears small green plantlets that drop off and propagate.

Habitat: Throughout the United States in fields, vacant lots, railroad rights-of-way, and other disturbed land.

Food uses: Always cook wild garlic and wild onions to cleave inulin molecules to a digestible sugar. Inulin is a polysaccharide, a stored-energy source typically found in roots and tubers and not easily digested. Taste a few bulbs in the spring, then eat the florets all summer.

Wild garlic

Medicinal uses: Wild garlic, chives, and onions may reduce blood pressure, lower cholesterol, lower blood sugar, and protect you from acute infections such as a cold or the flu.

WILD ONIONS AND CHIVES
Liliaceae (*Allium* spp.)

Nodding onion

Identification: Like wild garlic, onions and chives come early. Chives are some of the first flowers of spring, and they shoot up as tender rounded stems to 18" tall. Garlic leaves are flattened; chive and onion leaves are round.

Habitat: Disturbed ground, roadsides, fringes of lawns, fields, and meadows nationwide.

Food uses: Wild onion, field onions, wild chives, wild garlic, and wild leeks have edible flowers and edible bulbs. It is a good idea to cook the wild onion bulbs, as the inulin content is difficult for some people to digest. Cooking will break down this polysaccharide to a more manageable chain. After flowers bloom on these *Allium* species, a little bulblet, which is very edible, forms on the flower head. Pickle or stir-fry with vegetables and pork.

Medicinal uses: Like onion, garlic, and leek cultivars, wild alliums are infection fighters and may lower blood pressure. Sulfur compounds in alliums protect from acute infections like colds and flu. Like wild garlic, chives and onions reduce blood pressure, lower cholesterol, and stabilize or lower blood sugar.

WINTER CRESS; BLACK MUSTARD
Brassicaceae (*Barbarea vulgaris, Brassica nigra*)

Wild mustard

Identification: Both herbs are peppery tasting and have yellow flowers, with black mustard being preferred. Both have 4-petaled flowers, with black mustard flowers to ½" and winter cress to ⅓". Lower leaves of both plants divided into 5 segments (lobes), on winter cress with 4 lateral lobes and 1 terminal lobe; upper leaves on winter cress clasp stem, whereas upper leaves on black mustard are lance shaped, toothed, and not lobed.

Habitat: Fields, pastures, roadsides, and wetland edges nationwide.

Food uses: Eat the flowers and leaves. Allow a few flowers to go to seed for next year's crop. Greens come early, in March and April. Flowers are best early: April for winter cress, June for black mustard. Black mustard is a pleasant addition to salads and cooked greens.

Medicinal uses: Plants have isothiocyanates (antioxidants) hydrolyzed to sulforaphane in the mouth that provides protection from cancer.

YELLOW WOOD SORREL
Oxalidaceae *(Oxalis stricta)*

Wood sorrel

Identification: Small, low-lying plant that measures approximately 6"–15" in height. Easily recognizable by its light green, clover-shaped leaves. Flowers are small, delicate, and buttery yellow, ½" wide; 5 petals surround 10 stamens and a singular, erect central pistil. Flowers are widely spaced and moderate in number per plant. The clover-shaped leaves are small, approximately 0.6"–0.8" wide. Leaves are palmately divided into 3 distinct lobes and have a mildly sour taste. Leaves open at dawn and close at dusk or when exposed to environmental stresses. Each plant holds several leaves, creating a dense, carpet-like growth.

Habitat: Yards, gardens, vacant lots, roadsides.

Food uses: Yellow wood sorrel is also known as sour grass because its leaves have a mildly sour taste. Every part of this flower, including the leaves, flowers, and seedpods, is edible. Sorrel is a common addition to salads, soups, and sauces and can be used to make tea. Eat in moderation (see "Medicinal uses" below).

Note: Thrives where there is partial shade during the day, not full sunlight.

Medicinal uses: Contains vitamin C as well as potassium oxalate and oxalic acid, both of which can be hazardous to people with kidney disease, arthritis. Wood sorrel is cooling, diuretic; a digestive, astringent with blood-cleansing properties.

Fruit and Berries

APPLE AND CRAB APPLE (WILD APPLES)
Malvaceae (*Malus domestica, Malus spp.*)

Identification: Tree, 35' tall, cultivated and escaped to the wild; blossoms white to pink. Alternate ovate leaves, finely serrated. Crab apples are smaller, less than 1" wide in most cases, with ovate, serrated leaves (see photos).

Malus species

Habitat: Originally from central Asian temperate region, widely cultivated in the United States and has escaped to the wild. Found along roadsides and fringes of forests nationwide. Crab apples are the diminutive version of domesticated apples that have escaped cultivation. They are found along field and forest edges, woodlots, and road sides across much of the United States.

Crab apples fringing a marsh in Indiana

Food uses: Fresh, cooked, or dried fruit eaten. Also squeezed into cider and commercially produced as juice. Eating whole apples may lower cholesterol due to their high soluble-fiber content. Pinch a crab apple between thumb and forefinger and nibble around the seeds.

Medicinal uses: Parts used are the fruit, dried peels, flowers, and leaves. Dried peels used in teas. Apple leaf tea has a mild binding effect. Finely ground fruit and commercially prepared apple pectin used to treat diarrhea, stomach and bowel gas, and digestive complaints. Slice whole apples, peel and all, and dry in a food dehydrator. Eat several slices after an oily dinner to improve digestion and sequester cholesterol. This treat is very soothing to stomach distress and has a slight binding effect.

AUTUMN OLIVE
Elaeagnaceae (*Elaeagnus umbellata*)

Identification: Bush or shrub to 18' tall. Long, ovate leaves, toothless and leathery, width less than half the length, length usually ¾"–1½"; leaves silvery underneath. Leaves, twigs, and berries are speckled; yellow-white flowers cluster in leaf axils. Scarlet speckled berries about the size of a currant ripen in September.

Habitat: Edges of woods and fence-rows, in meadows, throughout the eastern United States and southern Canada; roadsides to the Missouri River.

Food uses: Eat out of hand. Simmer berries to juice, strain away seeds with a food mill or sieve. Reduce sauce; use over pancakes, waffles, wontons, and egg rolls. Jam recipe: 8 cups berries mixed with ½ cup agar flakes. Bring to a boil in a pan, stirring continuously.

Autumn olive

Lower heat, cover, and simmer for 15 minutes, stirring occasionally. Strain seeds and use as a freezer jam.

Medicinal use: Antiscorbutic (vitamin C content prevents scurvy).

BEARBERRY; UVA-URSI; KINNIKINNICK
Ericaceae *(Arctostaphylos uva-ursi)*

Identification: The plant is a trailing shrub, prostrate and mat forming. Leaves are dark, evergreen, leathery, smooth edged, obovate or spatula shaped, less than ¾" wide. Alpine variety of bearberry has larger leaves.

Habitat: I've found this plant in Michigan, Ontario, Oregon, Washington State, and British Columbia and

Bearberry

throughout the western and eastern mountain states.

Food uses: Leaves dried and mixed with tobacco for ritual Native American smoke. Berry is dry, mealy; was cooked with goose fat and other animal fats and eaten. Because of the berry's lack of flavor, mix with fish eggs and stronger-tasting foods to extend the nutrition. Dry berries in a food dehydrator and smash into flour-like substance. First People in the Northwest would use this flower like a spice on meat, liver. Leaves traditionally used in tea as a diuretic treatment for dropsy. Bella Coola tribe mixed berries in fat and ate them. Berries and leaves as a tea: tonic, diuretic, analgesic. Lower Chinook tribe dried berries then mixed them with fat for food. Native Americans boiled the berries with roots and vegetables to make a soup. First People ate the berries with fish eggs, preferably salmon eggs. Berries are sautéed in grease until crisp, then placed in cheesecloth (pantyhose will work) and pounded to break up berries. Add raw or cooked fish eggs and stir; pound to mix some more. Sweeten to taste.

Medicinal uses: Whole plant infused in water, then mixed with grease from a goose, duck, bear, or mountain goat and eaten. Infusion of aerial parts was gargled as mouthwash to treat canker sores and sore gums. Dried leaves and stems were ground and used as a poultice over wounds. Infusion of leaves, berries, and stems taken orally for cleaning kidneys and bladder complaints as a diuretic. Raw berries may be a laxative according to the Upper Tanana tribe. Raw leaves were chewed as a sialagogue to quench thirst when traveling. Infusion of the whole plant also taken to strengthen bones and bone breaks. Leaves and tobacco mixed and placed in all religious bundles for spiritual healing. Ritual smoking: leaves dried, toasted or roasted, crushed and smoked alone or mixed with tobacco. Pioneers considered the leaf infusion best known as diuretic, astringent, and tonic.

WARNING: Do not use during pregnancy and while nursing. Avoid acidic foods when using the tea to treat urogenital and biliary tract diseases. Prolonged use may damage liver and inflame and irritate bladder and kidneys. Not recommended for children.

BLACKBERRY
Rosaceae *(Rubus allegheniensis, R. laciniatus)*

Identification: Similar to raspberry. Shrub with spiny branches; compound leaves, 5+/– toothed leaflets (raspberry typically has 3 leaves); the white flower bloom appears after raspberries. *R. laciniatus* has sharply cut leaves. Blackberries found near your raspberry source. There are several species that ripen in mid- and late summer.

Blackberry

Habitat: Throughout the United States in fields, gardens, roadsides (more likely on side roads), fencerows, edges of woods.

Food uses: A low-calorie, high-nutrition breakfast made with blackberries: Mix 2 cups berries with 2 cups low-fat sweetened vanilla yogurt; add a dash of milk and blend—a wonderful ice-cream substitute with half the sugar and fat. Also use berries in pies, muffins, pancakes, jellies, and jams. Make tea from the leaves.

Medicinal uses: Native Americans used roots with other herbs for eye sores, backaches, and stomachaches. Pioneers made blackberry vinegar to treat gout and arthritis. The Chinese use *Rubus* species in a tea to stimulate circulation—they claim it helps alleviate pain in muscles and bones. Blackberries also contain several cancer-fighting antioxidants.

BLUEBERRY
Ericaceae (*Vaccinium myrtillus, Vaccinium* spp.)

Blueberry

Identification: Deciduous small shrub with sharp-edged green branches. Leaves alternate, simple smooth margin; flowers white to pink, tightly clustered. Flowers are about ¼" long, greenish, tinged with pale pink, containing 8–10 stamens, shorter than the styles. Globular fruit is blue-black, often frosted, with numerous tiny seeds dispersed through the purple pulp.

Habitat: Northern-tier states from coast to coast. Find them in Acadia National Park on the East Coast and as far west as Vancouver Island. Found in wetlands, lowlands, highlands including eastern and western mountains. Wild or cultivated found in every state of the union.

Food uses: Fruit eaten fresh or dried. Leaves made into tea. Freeze or dry for storage; keep dried berries in freezer. Stir frozen berries into desserts for an ice cream–like chill and texture. Use to make pies, muffins, pancakes, and waffles. Fold sour cream and blueberries into an omelet. Fruit antioxidant and a capillary protectant that may improve blood flow to distal areas (feet, brain, hands, etc.).

Medicinal uses: Native Americans used a decoction of fresh or dried berries to treat diarrhea. Iroquois used whole aerial part decoction as a topical application to dermatitis. Source of vitamin C. Dried pulverized leaves infused and taken for nausea. Folk use to prevent scurvy. Pioneers used leaves in decoction for treating diabetes. Berry tea used to treat mouth sores and inflammations.

CARRION FLOWER; SMOOTH CARRION FLOWER
Smilacaceae (*Smilax herbacea*)

Carrion flower

Identification: This is a climbing vine (to 8') or tangled bush without thorns. Flowers (May–June) are borne in round clusters and have a distinctive rotten odor.

Habitat: Grows in low, moist areas, margins of woods, roadsides, edges of wetlands, and meadows from Mason-Dixon Line north to Ontario, from the East Coast to the plains. Prefers rich, sandy loam. Pictured plant found 33' from lakeshore in northeast Indiana.

Note: Plant will come up in same location year after year.

Food uses: Berries are edible and remain on the plant throughout winter (although the longer you wait, the pulpier they get). Young shoots and leaves, like many others of the *Smilax* genus, are edible raw but unremarkable. Tuber is roasted, dried, and ground into flour—add to flour for pancakes, muffins, bread, waffles, and the like. If you are cross-country skiing through Michigan forests, *S. herbacea* is obvious against the white background, providing a pleasant trailside snack.

Medicinal uses: The *Smilax* genus has a long history of medicinal uses. Root decoction taken as an analgesic for backache. Crushed leaves rubbed over abrasions as an analgesic. Native Americans used parched and powdered leaves on inflammations and burns. Infusion of plant used to treat stomachache. Wilted leaves placed over boils. For further reference, see Daniel Moerman, *Native American Ethnobotany*.

CHERRIES: BLACK CHERRY AND CHOKECHERRY
Rosaceae *(Prunus serotina, P. virginiana)*

Black cherry

Identification: Bark of black cherry is rough, scaling. Peel the bark and the wood looks reddish underneath. Leaves ovate to lance shaped, toothed, smooth on top, midrib vein underneath has hairs. Leaf is also paler underneath. Berries are black, whereas chokecherries are reddish. Both berries hang from long, drooping racemes. Chokecherry is a smaller tree or shrub (black cherry may reach over 80'). Leaves are more oval with sharper teeth than black cherry leaf, with no hairs on midrib. White flowers on thicker raceme. Bark of black cherry when freshly torn is aromatic; chokecherry is not.

Chokecherry

Habitat: Cherry trees are typically a first-growth tree in the East, replaced by maple and beech. They are widespread in woods, even open places. Find chokecherry along streamsides in western dry areas—abundant along the Columbia River in Washington and the Clearwater River in Idaho.

Food uses: Bark, root, leaves inedible because of toxic glycoside prunasin, a hydrocyanic acid. Fruits of both plants are edible. Both make excellent jams, preserves. Put pitted cherries on cereal.

> **WARNING: Do not eat seeds. Fruit may be dried and frozen for later use as a trail food. Use only pharmaceutical-grade, professionally prepared formulations of this tree.**

Medicinal uses: Native Americans and pioneers used bark infusion as external wash. Black cherry: Inner bark used as a flavoring and therapeutic for colds, sore throats, diarrhea, respiratory infections and congestion, as well as inflammations, internally and externally.

CRANBERRY
Ericaceae *(Vaccinium oxycoccus)*

Cranberry

Identification: Evergreen, dwarf shrub that creeps through bogs on slender stems, occasionally rising 5"–15". Bark is hairy to smooth and brown to black in color. Pink flowers are nodding, with petals sharply bent backward like shooting stars. Flowers are either solitary or in couplets, rarely 3. Fruit color ranges from pink to red, depending on ripeness. Small berries are juicy and very tart.

Habitat: Hidden along the floor of sphagnum bogs, hummocks at low elevations (up to 6,000'–7,000'), including wet alpine meadows. They are widespread in acid bog habitats in the upper-tier states from coast to coast.

Food uses: Try it in your favorite apple crisp recipe, add black walnuts, and invite me over. Cranberries also spark up persimmon pudding. Dried cranberries good on pizzas, egg dishes, omelets, pancakes, oatmeal, waffles.

Medicinal uses: Berries and berry juice used as therapy for urinary tract infections—reported to acidify urine. Unverified claims suggest it helps remove kidney stones. Juice used to treat bladder infections and to prevent recurrence of urinary stones. It is antiscorbutic (has vitamin C to prevent or counteract scurvy). A study showed drinking the juice may prevent adhesion of *Escherichia coli* to gut lining and bladder lining. For detailed medicinal uses, see *Medicinal Plants of North America* (FalconGuides), by this author.

CURRANT
Grossulariaceae *(Ribes spp.)*

Golden currant, Absaroka-Beartooth Wilderness

Identification: A member of the large gooseberry family, with more than 30 species. Leaves are alternate and lobed 3–7 times with palmate veins. Flowers are small, solitary, in clusters, and variable in color, and have 5 petals smaller than sepals. Fruits are round, waxy, seeded, smooth or spiny; red, yellow, black, or purple. Gooseberries have spined berries, and currants are smooth. All are shrubs that can spread to 10' wide and 5' tall.

Habitat: Various species found from valley floor to 6,000'; typically the best locations are near streams and rivers, rockslides, burnouts, stream banks, and forests nationwide.

Food uses: Many currants are poor tasting—if the plant and fruit smells bad, it probably tastes the same. Eat out of hand, on breakfast cereals, in pancakes and waffles; dry or freeze the better-tasting fruits for later use.

Medicinal uses: A nontoxic fruit used as a panacea by Native Americans. The fruit contains ample amounts of gamma-linolenic acid (GLA), useful in treating a variety of illnesses, including diabetes, arthritis, alcoholism, eczema, and PMS.

ELDER, BLACK
Caprifoliaceae *(Sambucus canadensis)*

Elder

Identification: *Sambucus nigra* (introduced European variety and most studied) and *S. canadensis* are similar. Shrub or small tree to 25' in height; bark light brown to gray, fissured, and flaky. Branches break easily and die every autumn; when young they are green with gray lenticels. Leaves are matte green above and light blue-green underneath. Leaves are oblong, ovate, and serrated. White flowers and fruit are in large rounded clusters. Fruit is oval, black to deep violet.

Habitat: *S. canadensis* typically found in wet thickets, along edges of streams, rivers, and lakes. Numerous other species found coast-to-coast, typically in wet areas, along creeks, rivers, in lowlands, and mountains of the West.

Food uses: Use elder flowers and berries sparingly as food because safety is not universally established—eat at your own risk. I eat the white cluster of blossoms dipped in tempura batter (thin coating) then frittered. Sprinkle and serve as a health-protecting, heart-stimulating dessert. Cook berries then strain juice through a sieve; thicken with pectin to combine with jams and marmalades. Cooked juice also added to maple syrup. Juice, brown sugar, ginger, mustard, and soy combination provides a good wonton dip.

> **WARNING: Leaves and stems toxic—cyanide poisoning. Cook berries before consumption. The western variety with red berries may be more toxic than blue and black berries—avoid eating red elderberries.**

Medicinal uses: Flowers reported to lower fever and reduce inflammation and are alterative and diuretic when infused into tea. Tea used for influenza, colds, excess mucus, arthritis, asthma, bronchitis, improved heart function, fevers, hay fever, allergies, and sinusitis. Flowers infused in water and rubbed on skin soothe and soften irritations. Native Americans scraped bark and used root in infusion as emetic and laxative. Berry infusion used to treat rheumatism. Flower infusion induced sweats and used on colicky babies. Root pounded, decocted, and applied to swollen breasts; leaves in infusion as a wash for sores.

GOOSEBERRY, PRICKLY
Grossulariaceae *(Ribes cynosbati)*

Gooseberry

Identification: Shrub; spiny branches; spiny fruit, round to the size of a nickel in diameter, while its close relative, currant, has smooth or spiny fruit; deeply lobed leaves, sharply toothed; flowers yellow, purplish, or white (depending on species). You can find gooseberries and currants in woodlands and along the margins of woods. There are numerous species. The spiny, dangerous-looking berries are harmless and ready for harvest in early summer.

Habitat: Various species found throughout the United States in woodlands, along stream edges, and bordering wetlands.

Food uses: Make gooseberry-currant pie. Be certain to add lemon juice to punch up the taste. When fully ripe, eat out of hand, made into jams and jelly, and as a marinade ingredient for wild game and other cuts of meat.

Medicinal uses: Gooseberries and currants are made into a jelly spiced with peppermint, lemon juice, and ginger, then taken as a sore throat remedy. Some claim that gamma-linolenic acid (GLA), an active ingredient of currants, may prevent acne, obesity, and schizophrenia.

GRAPE, WILD
Vitaceae *(Vitis* spp.)

Identification: Climbing vine; clinging tendrils; green flowers in a large cluster; leaves alternate, simple, round, toothed, with heart-shaped base. The young leaves and ripe fruits are edible. Vines found clinging to and climbing trees, walls, and fences.

> **WARNING: The Canadian moonseed plant looks like wild grape but is poisonous. Learn to distinguish these 2 plants before eating what you think are wild grapes. Squash the moonseed fruit and look at the seed—see the crescent moon: Beware. Get expert identification.**

Habitat: Hardwood forest fringes and interior in eastern United States, roughly to Missouri.

Food uses: To make raisins, cover wild grapes with cheesecloth and dry them in the sun for 3 days, or dry them in a food dehydrator. Wrap grape leaves around rice, vegetables, and meat and steam until tender. Add grape leaves to pickling spices when preparing dill pickles.

Fox grape, Finger Lakes, New York

Poisonous moonseed

Medicinal uses: Fruit, leaves, and tendrils used by Native Americans and pioneers to treat hepatitis, diarrhea, and snakebites. Native Americans used tonic made with grape and several other herbs to increase fertility. Tannins and other phenolic compounds found in grape skins may provide protection from heart disease. Resveratrol from grapes may prevent strokes and heart attacks.

GROUND CHERRY; CHINESE LANTERN PLANT
Solanaceae *(Physalis* spp.)

Ground cherry

Identification: A member of the tomato family and close relative of the tomatillo, the ground cherry is similar to a tomato plant but stiffer and more erect. Either an annual or perennial, it has fuzzy leaves and bears a small tomato-like fruit enclosed in a papery husk that develops from the calyx.

Habitat: Prefers full sun; found along edges of gardens and vacant lots; species is tolerant of both cold and heat. Plant grows in poor and depleted soils, waste ground.

Food uses: Fruit is edible; mild flavor, with a hint of strawberry. Amish friends make them into pies with copious amounts of sugar (extra lemon juice necessary). Also eaten raw and in salads. Slice onto pizzas, add to sauces, chop into stews, and mix raw into mixed-fruit dishes. Use as a substitute for tomatillos in green salsa.

Medicinal uses: As a poultice over abscesses, a tea for coughs, and a drink for fevers and sore throats. Native Americans (Omaha) used *Physalis lanceolata* root decoction to treat headaches and stomachaches. Use with the oversight of a holistic health care practitioner.

HACKBERRY, COMMON
Cannabaceae/Ulmaceae
(*Celtis occidentalis*)

Identification: Tree grows to 50'; is rounded with grayish cork-like bark. Bark is tortured and replete with ridges and valleys—depressions to 3" deep. Leaves are ovate, alternate, coarse textured, toothed, asymmetrical, and pointed at the tip. Flower has 5 lobes, calyx with no petals, appears in May after leaves emerge. Small edible fruit is a drupe, fleshy and oblong, turning from orange-red to purple in the fall, and stays on the tree until desiccated. Sugar content becomes richer as berry ages. Old berries taste similar to a date.

Ridged bark of hackberry with coarse leaves

Fruit is sweet, tasty.

Habitat: Wide range of habitats; found with oaks and elms from the East Coast and across the United States to the prairie states, north to central Michigan and southern Ontario, south to Kentucky, Oklahoma, and west to South Dakota. It is, however, not common; seek guidance from locals and nature centers.

Food uses: Fruit is edible and sweet in the fall and best as a trail food. Seeds may be ground and used as a seasoning or flavoring to soups and roasted meat.

Medicinal uses: According to Daniel Moerman, *Native American Ethnobotany*, bark decoction used for treating a sore throat. Inner bark used to regulate menses.

Note: Hackberry seeds have been found in cave litter of Peking Man.

HAWTHORN
Rosaceae (*Crataegus laevigata*; more than 200 *Crataegus* species)

Identification: Shrubs to small trees, 6'–20'; many branched, branches thorned; leaves with 3–5 forward-pointing lobes, serrated leaf edges; leaves are yellow-green and glossy. White flowers are numerous, in terminal clusters, with 10–20 stamens, and give rise to small apple-like fruit. Fruit is

Hawthorn

ovoid to round, red or black, and mealy. There is 1 seed in each chamber of the ovary.

Habitat: *C. macrosperma* typically found east of the Mississippi in damp woods and fringes of forests; more rarely in western states. Other varieties found nationwide.

Food uses: Eaten out of hand, mealy and seedy, but heart-protecting value makes it worth the culinary failure. Fruit sliced and dried and decocted or infused in water to make a health-protecting drink; use with green tea. Berry has a sour to sweet flavor, and several varieties are bland. As a medicinal herb in Europe and China, hawthorn has long been used to treat heart disease. The active phytochemicals are bioflavonoids.

> ***WARNING: Extract may be a uterine stimulant, may induce menstruation; contraindicated for pregnant women.***

HIGH BUSH CRANBERRY
Caprifoliaceae *(Viburnum trilobum)*

High bush cranberry

Identification: Shrub with obvious 3-lobed compound leaf, leaf coarse and toothed (2"–4" long). Leaf lobes pointed. White flowers in flat clusters. Fruit turns red and is best after a frost or two.

Habitat: Roadsides, edges of marshes and thickets, lakeshores. Stands of these shrubs grow large and in profusion, with huge tart berries, along the coast of Lake Superior in the Pictured Rocks National Lakeshore (find them near the lighthouse).

Food uses: This is a Thanksgiving fruit, and I feel certain it was part of that first historic meal. The tart berries, best after a frost, go great in stuffing and marinades. They're made into jellies and infused into cold drinks. Remove seeds and simmer berries for best results—add sugar and lime juice, and reduce to a surprisingly fresh, tart, and delicious sauce.

Medicinal uses: Fruit is high in vitamin C. The plant is an escaped European gone wild. Fruit used in decoction to lower fevers. Bark decoction is a laxative and used to treat stomach cramps.

HUCKLEBERRY; EVERGREEN HUCKLEBERRY
Ericaceae *(Vaccinium ovatum)*

Identification: Bushy evergreen shrub to 7'. Twigs hairy, reddish in color; leaves evergreen, finely toothed, ½"–1" long, oval, thick, waxy; bell-shaped pink flowers. Blooms May–July depending on altitude and weather. Small, sweet, shiny black berries. Favorite bear food.

Habitat: Typically West Coast and mountain states from Alaska to California.

Food uses: Eat out of hand or in hot and cold cereals, or use to make jam. Marinade recipe: Simmer 1 cup berries; stir in 1 teaspoon Dijon mustard, 1 tablespoon soy sauce, 1 tablespoon crushed ginger, and the juice of half a lemon. Use marinade on salmon and chicken or as dip for wontons.

Medicinal uses: High in antioxidants, including anthocyanin. For diabetics, these berries may help manage blood-sugar levels.

Huckleberry

JUNEBERRY; SERVICEBERRY
Rosaceae *(Amelanchier spp.)*

Identification: Produces prodigious crops of fruit across North America. Various species are trees or shrubs. They have showy flowers, white to cream colored, drooping, with 5 lance-shaped petals. Leaves are oval, alternate, toothed—prominently at end of leaf—and entire or smooth toward the base. Fruit black to dark purple, 2 seeded, and juicy. Early April flowers in the Midwest, later in the Mountain West. Fruits available all summer depending on longitude and latitude.

Juneberry flower

Habitat: The plant prefers moist soil or rocky areas, fringes of wooded areas and near water sources, from sea level to alpine elevations. *Amelanchier alnifolia* grows in profusion along the Columbia River in Washington and along the Clearwater and Selway Rivers in Idaho. At Hyalite Reservoir, the South Shore Trail shares the fruit with you.

Juneberry fruit

Food uses: Berry is edible and a welcome addition to pancakes, waffles, muffins, and game dishes (venison or buffalo). Try them with breakfast cereal. Cook berries down with honey or maple syrup to make preserves; add lemon or lime juice. Mix with huckleberries and other fruit for field berry pie. Cambium of shrub considered nutritious and given to Native American babies.

Medicinal uses: Native Americans boiled berries and used decoction as an antiseptic, typically for earaches and colds. Teething babies sipped on a decoction of the roots. Sharpened twigs used to puncture pustules on people and animals. Boiled bark taken for stomachaches.

JUNIPER
Cupressaceae *(Juniper communis)*

Juniper communis

Identification: An evergreen tree or low-lying, spreading shrub, often in colonies. It has flat needles in whorls of 3, spreading from the branches. Leaves are evergreen, pointy, stiff, somewhat flattened and light green, some say sea green. Buds are covered with scalelike needles. Berries are blue, hard, and when scraped with a fingernail, they emit a tangy smell and impart a tangy flavor—a somewhat creosote-like taste. Male flowers are catkin-like with numerous stamens in 3 segmented whorls. Female flowers are green and oval.

Habitat: Found across the United States. Often found in dune blowouts along the shore of Lake Michigan and throughout eastern and western mountains. It easily relocates to gardens and yards.

Food uses: Cook dried berries with game and fowl. Try putting them in a pepper mill and grating them into bean soup, stews, on wild game and domestic fowl. To make berries into tea, simply crush 2 berries and add to hot water or to green tea just off the boil. Juniper berries infused into vodka to flavor it. Gin, schnapps, and aquavit also flavored with juniper berries. Berries also used in grilling marinades. When grated it is added to cold cuts. Try it as a spice on vegetated protein cold cuts, like Wham and mock chicken, garden burgers. Large amounts of the berry may be toxic—use in small amounts like a spice.

Medicinal uses: Native Americans used juniper branches around tepees and shelters to fend off rattlesnakes. The diluted essential oil applied to skin to draw and cleanse deeper skin tissue. A few holistic practitioners use juniper berries to promote menstruation to relieve premenstrual syndrome and dysmenorrhea. Traditional practitioners use 1 teaspoon of berries to 1 cup of water, boil for 3 minutes, let steep until cool. Some practitioners add bark and needles to berry tea. The berry is antiseptic, diuretic, a tonic, and a digestive aid—strongly antiseptic to urinary tract problems and gallbladder complaints, but contraindicated for kidney disease.

WARNING: Avoid during pregnancy. The herb may induce contractions and may increase menstrual bleeding. Do not use if kidney infection or kidney disease is suspected. Do not use the concentrated and caustic essential oil internally.

MAYAPPLE

Berberidaceae *(Podophyllum peltatum)*

Identification: Large pair of dissected, parasol-like leaves; white flower on petiole between leaves; yellow-green fruit. Mayapple parts are, for the most part, poisonous. The 2 large, parasol-like leaves shelter a white flower that bears an edible fruit when ripe in midsummer. Pick the fruit when soft and ripe.

Mayapple

Habitat: Forest-dwelling plant, found in most states except extreme desert, southern California, and lower Florida.

Food uses: Expert foragers carefully gather ripe fruit for use in pie fillings and jellies. Fruit ripe in late June or July, but hurry—every raccoon and its friends are competing with you.

Mayapple fruit

WARNING: Except for the pulp of the ripe fruit, this plant is poisonous.

Medicinal uses: An analog of etoposide, the active agent of mayapple, is used to treat testicular and small-cell lung cancer.

MOUNTAIN ASH

Rosaceae *(Sorbus sitchensis, S. americana)*

Identification: Shrub or small tree to 40'. Compound leaves, 11–17 toothed leaflets; leaves long and narrow, 3 times longer than broad; flowers and fruit in rounded clusters. Berries are red when ripe, best after a frost.

Habitat: *S. sitchensis* is found in the western United States, at higher elevations and moist areas. *S. americana* is found in northern tier of the eastern states, typically around moist areas; abundant along the coast of Lake Superior.

Food uses: Berries are best after a frost (or you can freeze, thaw, and then eat them). Their high pectin content makes them a good addition to preserves and jellies. Mix about ¼ cup mountain ash berries to 1 cup blueberries or cherries. Use boiled berries, sweetened to taste, as relish for meat; very good over goose and duck. Green or ripe fruit may be mashed and used to marinate meat.

Medicinal uses: Native Americans used the inner bark and gummy terminal buds of *S. americana* as a tonic. The tonic is reported to enhance mood and treat depression. Bark and bud infusion is considered antimicrobial and an appetite stimulant. Inner bark and/or gummy red terminal buds infused for colds. Inner bark infusion

Mountain ash berries

Mountain ash in bloom

used to reduce pain after childbirth; root infusion used to treat colic. Root and bark decoction used for treating rheumatism and arthritis. Wood ash is styptic and considered useful for treating burns and boils. Root of sweet flag and *S. americana* were combined and infused as spring tonic. Berries used as a digestive aid. Twigs of western species used as chewing stick (toothbrush).

MULBERRY
Moraceae *(Morus nigra)*

Identification: Small to medium-size tree. Leaves are simple, alternate, toothed, round, or slightly elongated, broadest near the base. Flowers green, tiny, clustered on a spike. Berry varieties are red, white, and black. Berry juicy, sweet and soft when ripe. Berry looks similar to a blackberry but more elongated.

Black mulberry

Habitat: Primarily east of the Mississippi, frequent along roadsides, fencerows, lakeshores. Widely distributed by birds.

Food uses: Trail food, put on cereals, flavor fudge. Unripe fruit is said to be mildly hallucinogenic. I have never experienced that and have eaten plenty—one of my favorite fruits. Very abundant. Can be frozen and used in cocktails; mixed with other berries in pies, cobblers.

Medicinal uses: Mulberries contain high amounts of iron and vitamin C.

OREGON GRAPE
Berberidaceae (*Mahonia aquifolium, M. nervosa*)

Identification: To 6' tall (*M. aquifolium*) evergreen shrub, with shiny holly-like leaves; leaves leathery, pinnate, compound, with pointed edges. Flower is small, bright yellow. Berries deep blue, waxy. Gray stem. Roots and root hairs, when peeled, are bright yellow inside due to alkaloid berberine. *M. nervosa* is a smaller forest dweller up to 3' tall with a rosette of compound leaves in a whorl; berries on central spikes.

Mahonia aquifolium

Habitat: *M. nervosa* found in open forests and graveyards, with numerous sites along Mount Baker Highway in Washington en route to Mount Baker. *M. aquifolium* is found along roadsides, forest edges from Washington State into Idaho and Montana.

Mahonia nervosa

Food uses: Tart berries of *M. aquifolium* eaten in late summer. Native Americans smashed the berries and dried them for later use. They may be boiled with ample amounts of sugar into jam (or honey); the juice is tart. Carrier Indians of the Northwest simmered young leaves and ate them. The smaller creeping *M. nervosa* is prepared and eaten in the same way and is preferred but not as abundant. Try berries mixed with other fruit to improve taste. Berries are pounded to paste, formed into cakes, and dried for winter food.

Medicinal uses: When eaten raw in small amounts, the fruit is slightly emetic. Tart berries of both species considered a morning-after pick-me-up. A decoction of stem used as an antiemetic. These 2 bitter and astringent herbs are used in decoction to treat liver and gallbladder complaints. The bark infusion was used by Native Americans as an eyewash. According to traditional use, the decocted drug from the inner bark (berberine) stimulates the liver and gallbladder, cleansing them, releasing toxins, and increasing the flow of bile. *M. aquifolium* extractions are available in commercial ointments to treat dry skin, unspecified rashes, and psoriasis. Do not use during pregnancy. The bitter drug may prove an appetite stimulant, but little research has been done. Other unproven uses in homeopathic doses include the treatment of liver and gallbladder problems.

Note: The shredded bark and roots of both species can also be simmered in water to make a bright yellow dye.

PAWPAW
Annonaceae *(Asimina triloba)*

Identification: Small tree (10'–25')
growing on riverbanks, along streams;
as a secondary growth under taller
trees, loves shade, does not tolerate
sunlight. Leaves are alternate, simple,
large (up to 12"), narrow at base and
broad near tip. Flowers are elegant,
large, and come early; worth the trip
into the woods.

Pawpaw

Habitat: Eastern and southern United
States growing beneath hardwoods
with numerous stands along the south-
eastern shore of Lake Michigan, just
beyond the fringing dunes.

Food uses: Large fruit eaten raw, or
remove seeds and cook like pudding
and then blend with yogurt. Pawpaw
shakes blended with other berries are
delicious and nutritious. Freeze fruits
for future use. Let unripe fruits ripen in
vegetable drawer of a refrigerator; once
ripe, however, they spoil quickly.

Pawpaw flower

Medicinal use: An anticancer substance has been isolated from pawpaw that is
more than 1,000 times as potent as the synthetic drug Adriamycin.

PERSIMMON
Ebenaceae *(Diospyros virginiana)*

Identification: A small to medium (to
60') irregularly shaped tree with gray
or black bark arranged in a blocky
(mosaic) pattern with orange in the
valleys between the blocks. Lateral
branches are typically much smaller in
diameter than the trunk. Flowers are 4
lobed and yellow. Leaves are stiff, oval,

Persimmon

alternate, and smooth edged. Fruit is orange, pulpy, and retains the flower's calyx;
soft and darkens when ripe—astringent when unripe, sweet when ripe.

Habitat: Edges of woods, cultivated arboretums; tolerates dryness, prefers well-
drained soil. Persimmon trees found as far north as the protected temperate areas
of the Great Lakes. Lower Michigan is the upper limit of this tree's range.

Food uses: Leaves make a refreshing tea. Native Americans fermented this fruit in water to make an alcoholic drink—roll fruit in cornmeal and soak in water to ferment. Fruit is edible late in the season when the cold takes the "pucker" off its taste. Pudding made from the fruit is delicious. Collect fruit after a frost, when it is soft and sweet. Best picked off the ground; then you know it is ready.

Persimmon fruit

Medicinal uses: Syrup made from unripe fruit said to be therapeutic treatment of diarrhea. Astringency of the fruit may explain this use. Infusion of the bark used to treat liver problems (folk and Native American tradition). Astringency of fruit made for a sore throat gargle after infusing mashed fruit in water. Bark chewed for gastrointestinal stress, acid reflux of the stomach.

RASPBERRY
Rosaceae *(Rubus idaeus, R. occidentalis)*

Identification: Shrub with spiny branches; compound leaves, 3–5 leaflets, sharply toothed; white flowers, 3 or more petals. Berry pulls free from stem and has a hollow center.

Habitat: Red and black raspberries found along the fringes of woods, fencerows, and the margins of fields. Berries are ready for harvest in late spring and early summer throughout the United States.

Raspberry (numerous species)

Food uses: Use as pie filling, or stir into pancake batter and muffin mixes. Makes excellent jam or jelly.

Medicinal uses: Leaves are steeped as tea and used as a tonic for pregnant women. Native Americans used root for diarrhea and dysentery. Also used to flavor medicines. Like other berries, it's a great dietary choice for weight watchers—it's high in cancer-fighting ellagic acid. One cup of raspberries per day shows promise as an anticancer agent. Nonanone, the frosty appearance of wild raspberries, is an antifungal agent that protects the berries from fungal infections. That's why wild raspberries do not spoil as quickly as cultivars that have lost their capacity to produce nonanone.

ROSES, WILD
Rosaceae *(Rosa* spp.*)*

Rose

Identification: Typically a sprawling or climbing shrub with thorns, conspicuous flowers; famous for the rose hip, its fruiting body. Leaves are ovate, finely serrated.

Habitat: Widespread and numerous species from coast to coast.

Food uses: Flower petals are edible, as is the fruiting body. Flower petals candied: Mix high-proof grain alcohol with sugar until hypertonic solution (sugar no longer dissolves in solution). Paint rose with sugar-alcohol solution and let dry. Extract rose water from rose petals with an inexpensive over-the-counter still. See our DVD *Cooking with Edible Flowers and Culinary Herbs* for details (it's listed in appendix C: "References and Resources"). Rose water flavors desserts, piecrusts, chicken dishes.

Medicinal uses: Rose water used as a wash to protect the skin; fruits eaten as a source of vitamin C and to stem diarrhea; bark tea drunk for dysentery. A decoction of bark imbibed to treat worms; root tea as eyewash. Floral tea used by this author as stimulant and tonic. It may promote improved circulation, reduce rheumatic pain, stem dysentery, and relieve stomachache. Petal infusion may relieve inflammation of the mouth and pharynx.

SALAL
Ericaceae *(Gaultheria shallon)*

Salal

Identification: Sprawling shrub forms dense thickets in northwestern pine forests. Oval, shiny, leathery, thick leaves are alternate, clinging to sturdy stems on petioles of varying lengths. Bell-shaped pink to white flowers strung out like pearls near ends of stem. Dark blue to blue-black fruit is ripe July–September.

Habitat: Seashore west of the Cascades and coastal ranges; under Douglas fir and cedar from California to the Alaskan peninsula.

Food uses: Eat the berries as you hike along. Take some home and blend them into jelly or maple syrup, or dry them in a food dehydrator and use them in muffins, waffles, or pancakes. Another tasty addition to marinades; berries also used to make wine.

Medicinal uses: Native Americans chewed the leaves to stem hunger. Dried salal berries are considered laxative, while the plant's dried leaves infused in water can be imbibed to treat diarrhea (the tea is astringent). Dried leaves powdered and used externally as a styptic on scrapes and abrasions. Also, dried leaf powder mixed with water to make a pasty poultice for wounds.

SALMONBERRY
Rosaceae *(Rubus spectabilis)*

Salmonberry

Identification: Shrub 6'–7' in height, found along moist slopes, sunny banks, and streams. Brown stems with yellow bark, laced with weak-to-soft thorns; leaflets fuzzy with serrated edges, usually in 3s, approximately 3" in length. Fuchsia flowers arrive with leaves in spring. Soft, dry fruit ranges from bright red to yellowish.

Note: I find this berry on Vancouver Island along the path to Botanical Beach.

Habitat: Moist edges of woods, seeps, edges of meadows, streamsides from Michigan west to the Sierras; Rockies north to Alaska.

Food uses: The soft (when ripe) fruit melts in your mouth and will melt in your backpack, too—best eaten as you hike along. Spring sprouts peeled, cooked, and eaten. Harvest the stems before they become hard and woody, and eat them raw, steamed, or roasted.

Medicinal uses: Root bark decoction taken for stomach ailments. Poultice of bark applied to toothache. For further reference, see Daniel Moerman's *Native American Ethnobotany*.

SPICEBUSH
Lauraceae *(Lindera benzoin)*

Spicebush

Identification: Shrub found in rich woodlands and along streams. Grows to 15', with numerous spreading branches. Smooth branches give off spicy odor when soft bark is scratched with thumbnail. Leaves smooth, bright green, pointed (widest near or above middle section), simple, alternate, deciduous, 2½"–5½" long and 1½"–2½" wide. Flowers small, yellow, in dense clusters along previous year's twigs. Fruits in clusters, widest in middle (somewhat football shaped but with more rounded ends); start out green and become bright red in autumn. Flowers appear in early spring, before leaves.

Habitat: Eastern United States, roughly to the Mississippi River. In rich, moist forest as understory in birch, beech, and hardwood forest.

Food uses: In the spring gather end twigs, tie them together with string, and throw them in a pot with leeks, nettles, mushrooms, and dandelions. Bundles of stems can be steeped in boiling water to make tea (sweeten with honey). Young leaves can be used in the same way. In the fall try drying the fruits in a food dehydrator. Dry fruits are hard and can be ground in a coffee mill and used as a substitute for allspice. Fruits used in meat marinades. Try it with your ribs recipe—like juniper berries, 3–5 berries are sufficient. Chew green end twigs as a chew stick while you walk to freshen your mouth and cleanse your teeth.

Medicinal uses: Native Americans used the bark in infusion for treating colds, coughs, and dysentery. Tea made from the bark was used as a spring tonic. Bathing in this tea reportedly helps rheumatism. Tea made from the twigs was used to treat dysmenorrhea.

STAGHORN SUMAC
Anacardiaceae *(Rhus typhina)*

Staghorn sumac

Identification: Shrub or small tree; leaves lance shaped, alternate, compound, numerous leaflets, toothed; cone-shaped flower and berry clusters. The large berry spikes of staghorn sumac are ready to harvest in late summer.

Habitat: Entire United States except extreme desert, southern California, and lower Florida.

Food uses: Strip ripe (red) staghorn sumac berries from heads. Discard stems and heads. Soak "cotton"-covered berries in hot water to extract a lemonade-like drink. Steep sassafras root in the tea. Add sugar and serve.

Medicinal uses: Staghorn sumac flower can be steeped into tea and taken for stomach pain. Gargles made from berries are purported to help sore throats.

STRAWBERRY
Rosaceae *(Fragaria virginiana, F. vesca, F. californica)*

Strawberry

Identification: White flower; sharply toothed leaflets in 3s, growing in colonies; looks like the store-bought variety but smaller.

Habitat: *F. virginiana* found in the eastern United States, roughly to the

Mississippi; *F. vesca* found west of the Mississippi River; and *F. californica* found in California and Baja. Look for strawberries in meadows and open woods. Harvest in late May and early June.

Food uses: Strawberries are high in vitamin C and are fiber rich—a good choice for dieters. A wet spring will bring a robust harvest. Use on cereals, with yogurt, on pancakes and waffles, in summer drinks, and with ice cream.

Medicinal uses: Native Americans used strawberries to treat gout, scurvy, and kidney infections. Root tannins were used to treat malaria. The fruits contain ellagic acid.

THIMBLEBERRY
Rosaceae *(Rubus parviflorus)*

Identification: Deciduous shrub up to 7' high, barbless stems, erect with shredded to smooth bark. Leaves are large, maplelike, smooth or slightly hairy on top, fuzzy underneath. Picked berry fits on your finger like a thimble.

Habitat: Found in moist places (streamside, lakeside, and coastal)—Mountain West, primarily the Sierras and Rockies to Alaska.

Ripe and unripe thimbleberry

Food uses: Eat the soft, ripe berries in the bush. Like salmonberry (see above), thimbleberry will turn to mush in your backpack. To eat: Apply forefinger and thumb to fruit, pull and twist, and pop in your mouth. No cooking required. Try this tart berry on cereal. Northwestern Native Americans dried the berries in cakes or stored them in goose grease. Young shoots harvested, peeled, and cooked as a spring green.

Medicinal uses: Kwakiutl nation of the Northwest made a decoction, a boiled drink for treating bloody vomiting, that included blackberry roots, vines, and thimbleberry.

WINTERGREEN; SPOTTED WINTERGREEN
Ericaceae *(Gaultheria procumbens, Chimaphila maculata)*

Identification: Evergreen; long oval leaves, finely serrated margins; drooping white flowers. The flower forms an edible berry that turns from white to red by late summer. Available all winter—if not gobbled up by late-season foragers.

Habitat: Entire United States except extreme desert, southern California, and lower Florida. There are several species of this plant in North America. Creeping wintergreen, or checkerberry, found in the eastern half of the United States.

Wintergreen

Spotted wintergreen

Food uses: Add summer fruits to pancake and muffin mixes. Use the leaves to make a delicate tea, or munch them (don't swallow) as a breath freshener.

Medicinal uses: Astringent, counterirritant. Never take oil internally. Tea from leaves used for flu and colds and as a stomach alkalizer. Analgesic and rubefacient oil for muscular pain and arthritic pain; also a flavoring agent for cough drops.

Wetlands

AMERICAN LOTUS
Nelumbonaceae *(Newlumbo lutea)*

American lotus

Identification: A perennial plant often confused with water lilies; like water lilies, can form large colonies in sluggish or still water. Flowers are to 10" wide, yellowish-white to yellow with more than 20 petals. The seed-holding head looks a bit like an upside-down shower head. Seeds are the size of a green pea. Leaves are simple, round, bluish-green in color, leaf size variable up to 2' in diameter, conical when emerging in the spring and flat in the summer, rising as high as 4" above water on a rigid stem. Edible tuber is a rhizome.

Habitat: Swamps, lakes, sluggish water with muddy bottoms. Often found above dams on the Mississippi River.

Food uses: Seed and rhizome are edible. Both the seed and root are best cooked. I have not had the luxury to try this. If you have, please join me on Facebook and report your experience.

Medicinal uses: Juice of the root used by Native Americans to treat colds. Dried and powdered root reconstituted with water and sucked to relieve mouth sores. Root is tannin rich and can be used with water to gargle for irritation of the mouth and/or throat. Decoction of root used to treat vaginal disorders. For more see *Medicinal Plants of North America*, FalconGuides, by this author.

Note: Find American lotus just north of the US Army Corps of Engineers dam on the Illinois side of the Rock River near Moline.

AMERICAN WATER LILY
Nymphaeaceae *(Nymphaea odorata)*

Water lily

Identification: Large white flower to 5" in diameter with numerous petals and yellow reproductive parts; roots submerged in fresh water; leaves flat, platter shaped, 6"–10" across.

Habitat: Found floating on still or gently moving shallow water to 3' in depth. Found across the northern tier of states, farther south in the East, and rarely in the Southwest.

Food uses: Eat the unfurled leaves of spring and unopened flower buds. Wash petals and cook to remove potential larvae and other aquatic pests.

Medicinal uses: Dried and powdered root sucked in mouth to relieve mouth sores. Juice of root used to treat colds. Numerous tribes used the root juice, decoction, and powdered roots in many ways, primarily to treat colds and coughs.

ARROWHEAD; WAPATO; DUCK POTATOES
Alismataceae *(Sagittaria latifolia)*

Wapato

Identification: Arrow-shaped leaves, widely and deeply cleft, veins palmate; white, platter-shaped flowers with 3 petals; deep-set tube growing up from a soft bottom.

Habitat: Edges of slow-moving streams, ponds, and along shorelines of lakes with soft bottom edges; ranges across northern tier of states, from Maine to Washington.

Food uses: Harvest tuber in fall or early spring. Boil until tender, pluck away skin, and sauté or smash and cook like hash browns. Native Americans roasted the tubers, peeled them, and ate out of hand.

Medicinal uses: Root said to settle the stomach, alleviate indigestion. Poultice of root applied to cuts and abrasions.

CATTAILS
Typhaceae *(Typha angustifolia, T. latifolia)*

T. latifolia (left 2 leaves) and *T. angustifolia* (right 2 leaves)

Identification: Wetland grass with long sword-shaped leaves, 2-headed flower, male spike on top and female just below. Grows to 7'; flower heads develop in May and June, later in the mountain states.

Habitat: Numerous species worldwide. Broadleaf (*T. angustifolia*) and narrow leaf (*T. latifolia*) are common across the central and northern-tier states. Found along streams, in marshes, fens, bogs, and other wetlands with still or slow-moving water.

Food uses: Collect the male flowering parts in late May–June in Michigan, about 2–3 pounds, and then freeze. Add the male parts to pizza dough, bread dough, cookies, and biscuits—anything you bake—to enrich the final product with essential amino acids and bioflavonoids. Strip young shoots (through June) of their tough outer leaves down to the delicate core. Eat on the spot, or sauté or stir-fry. Roots are starch rich and provide needed energy for beavers, muskrats, and humans. The young (June) female flower spike is boiled and eaten like corn on the cob. Alas, it does not taste like corn on the cob, but once again, it may be the difference between starving and survival.

Cattail pollen

Medicinal uses: The mucilaginous chopped root is applied to wounds, minor abrasions, inflammations, and burns. Burned cattail ash is styptic and used to stop bleeding and disinfect wounds.

Note: Dried cattail fluff is an excellent fire accelerator; use in the fire nest.

CHUFA SEDGE; YELLOW NUT SEDGE
Cyperaceae *(Cyperus esculentus)*

Chufa sedge

Identification: Green flower with numerous spikes. Grows to 3', with flat seeds surrounded by 4 bracts at 90 degrees to one another; leaves are slender, tough, grasslike (but not a grass), and grow from an underground tuber.

Habitat: In or near wetlands, escaped to gardens—prefers damp soil. Found coast-to-coast, in all states except perhaps Montana and Wyoming.

Food uses: Roots dried, ground, and cooked with other food; or simply dig roots, wash, and eat raw. They are also baked or boiled.

Medicinal uses: Pima and other tribes chewed roots to treat colds.

CINQUEFOIL
Rosaceae (*Potentilla canadensis, P. anserina*)

Cinquefoil

Identification: Leaves on long, jointed stolons (delicate stemlike appendages). Two types of leaves: oval or elliptical (which are much smaller and have sharply toothed leaflets up to 1¼" long), with small buttercup-like flower.

Habitat: *P. canadensis* found in the eastern United States to the Mississippi in fields, waste ground, roadsides, and meadows. Both species can be found on waste ground or in gravelly or sandy habitats.

Food uses: *P. canadensis* is used to make a gold-colored tea that is high in calcium. For a quick roast, cook the leaves in a hot (covered) Dutch oven for 2–3 minutes or pour boiling water over the leaves. *P. anserina* roots are edible. Gather the roots, wash them thoroughly, and steam in a wok. Native Americans steamed the roots in cedar boxes and served them with duck fat. To this day the Ditidaht peoples of British Columbia gather and prepare the roots in this traditional way.

Medicinal uses: Roots are rich in tannins and are used by some naturopathic physicians to treat diarrhea, Crohn's disease, colitis, gastritis, and peptic ulcers. Use only under the supervision of a trained holistic health-care practitioner.

DUCKWEED
Lemnaceae (*Lemna trisulca*)

Duckweed

Identification: One of the smallest flowering plants, it covers still water and turns pond surfaces green by early summer—from a distance it looks like green pond scum. Up close it is a single or double leaf floating on the surface of the water, with 2 root hairs siphoning nutrients from the water. It is the habitat of many larval forms of life, so cooking is imperative. Size: smaller than the nail on your pinky, to ½".

Habitat: Surface of still fresh water. Found coast-to-coast.

Food uses: Thoroughly wash, then cook in soups and stews. What I consider a survival food, and there is plenty of it. Its texture is crunchy, especially if larval snails are not removed from the food.

Medicinal uses: In poultice and applied to swellings and inflammations.

HAIRY BITTERCRESS
Brassicaceae *(Cardamine hirsuta)*

Hairy bittercress

Identification: Plant borne from a rosette of pinnately divided (lobed) leaves with 8–15 leaflets on short stem. Stem is either unbranched or branched near the base. Flowers presented on an erect stem. Small (¼"+/–) white flowers (4 petals, 4 sepals). Flower is spatula shaped; has 4 stamens in contrast to similar cress with 6 stamens. Edible flowers in spring and fall are best to collect. Plant may flower in 2 seasons depending on latitude and severity of winters. Seeds are dispersed mechanically: popped and thrown from the parent plant and widely dispersed—dispersion process is called ballochory. Similar species, *C. flexuosa*, has 6 stamens and stem-clasping leaves.

Habitat: Widely dispersed in the United States in lawns, disturbed ground, edges of meadows, and open areas, even turf-growing areas and wetlands. Look in areas of partial shade.

Food uses: Early flowers and leaves edible in salads and soups and cooked dishes. See Hairy Cress Scramble recipe in appendix B.

Medicinal uses: Not much in the literature. Like other members of the mustard family, it contains cancer-inhibiting compounds: vitamin C, beta-carotene, and other antioxidants.

Note: Can be very bitter; cooking helps reduce bitterness. Plant often found in substantial amounts. Collect early in season.

HORSETAIL; SCOURING RUSH; EQUISETUM
Equisetaceae *(Equisetum hyemale, E. arvense)*

Equisetum

Identification: The plant my brother and I called snakeweed when kids, the segmented stem can be pulled apart and put back together at the joints to make necklaces and bracelets. It appears in the spring as a naked segmented stem with a dry-tipped sporangium with spores. Later the sterile stage stems arise with many long needlelike branches arranged in whorls up the stem.

Habitat: Found around marshes, fens, bogs, streams, lakes, rivers, and in my garden.

Food uses: Native Americans of the Northwest eat the tender young shoots of the plant as a blood purifier (tonic). The tips (the strobili) are boiled and eaten in Japan: Mix vinegar and soy; boil shoots in vinegar for 5 minutes and enjoy. Native Americans of the Southwest eat the roots.

Medicinal uses: Mexican Americans use dried whole aerial plant parts of horsetail in infusion or decoction to treat painful urination. Therapy not supported by scientific evidence. But equisetonin and bioflavonoids in the plant may account for its diuretic effect. Native Americans used a poultice of the stem to treat rashes of the armpit and groin, and an infusion of the stem was used by Blackfeet as a diuretic. Cherokee used aerial part infusion to treat coughs in their horses. Infusion of the plant used to treat dropsy, backaches, cuts, and sores. Baths of the herb reported to treat syphilis and gonorrhea. This is one of the First People's most widely used herbs.

JEWELWEED; SPOTTED TOUCH-ME-NOT
Balsaminaceae *(Impatiens capensis)*

Jewelweed

Identification: Fleshy annual of wetlands to 7' in height. Simple green, almost translucent stems with swollen nodes. Deep green leaves are thin, ovate, with 5–14 teeth. Plants grow in dense colonies, often with stinging nettle. Flowers are orange-yellow with reddish-brown spots. They are spur shaped and irregular, with the spur curving back and lying parallel to the sac. Flower is about ½" wide and ¾" in length. Fruit is oblong capsule that, when ripe, bursts open and disperses the seeds.

Habitat: Lowlands, wetlands, edges of lakes and streams, wet fens, edges of bogs, and relocates to the garden, providing food and medicine. Young shoots of spring form a complete ground cover in wet lowlands, along streams, wetlands, lakes.

Food uses: Eat the small flowers of summer in salads and stir-fries. Pick the young shoots of spring and add to your mushroom soup, egg dishes, or stir-fry, or sauté with spring vegetables.

Medicinal uses: Traditional treatment for poison ivy. Crush and rub the aerial parts of plants over inflamed area of dermatitis for an immediate anti-inflammatory effect, reducing itching and inflammation. The Creek tribe used an infusion of smashed spicebush berries and jewelweed as a bath for congestive heart failure. Crushed flowers used on bruises, cuts, and burns. Repeated applications of the juice may remove warts. Whole herb infused as an appetite stimulant and diuretic. Used by naturopaths to treat dyspepsia.

LABRADOR TEA
Ericaceae (*Ledum groenlandicum, L. glandulosum*)

Labrador tea

Identification: Evergreen shrub 15"–30" or more; flowers with 5 petals (⅜" wide) that form flat terminal clusters; fruits in round nodding capsules—leaves evergreen, oval to lance shaped down rolled edges, woolly underneath.

Habitat: Found in boggy areas of the western mountains and northern tier of eastern states and southern Canadian provinces.

Food uses: Leaves and flowers are used to make tea. Labrador tea is preferred over glandular Labrador tea, which is slightly toxic and mildly narcotic, causing stomach distress and even death from an overdose. Be careful, as these species can be confused with bog laurels.

Medicinal uses: Native Americans used the leaf and floral tea to treat acute infections such as colds and sore throats. Smoking the dried leaves was claimed to induce euphoria. Crushed and powdered leaves were used as snuff to treat inflammation of the nasal passages. Tea said to help alleviate allergies. The tea is diuretic, laxative, and a smooth-muscle relaxant. According to Kershaw in *Edible and Medicinal Plants of the Rockies*, crushed leaves used by Scandinavians to flavor schnapps—the alcoholic nightcap is used as a sleep aid. Alcohol extracts used to treat numerous skin conditions, including inflammation, scabies, fungus, and chigger and lice bites. Powdered roots were applied to ulcers. Fresh leaves are chewed as a general tonic.

MINT; PEPPERMINT
Lamiaceae (*Mentha piperita, M. aquatica*)

Peppermint

Identification: There are many American members of the mint family. The genus has several characteristics in common: a square stem, almost always aromatic when crushed, typically aggressive and spreading. Flowers are in dense whorls culminating in a terminal spike of blossoms that crown the stem, or in the leaf axils. Color varies by species—white, violet, blue. The root is a spreading rhizome with erect stems. Leaves are ovate to roundish and elongated in a few species, typically serrated.

Habitat: *Mentha aquatica* and *M. piperita* can usually be found around water, shorelines, stream banks, dunes of the Great Lakes, and mountain passes; blowdowns, avalanche slides, and wet meadows.

Food uses: Leaves in teas, salads, cold drinks, sautéed vegetables; wonderful in Mexican bean soups and as an integral part of the subcontinent and Middle Eastern flavor principles.

Medicinal uses: Leaf and flower infusion (or the extracted oil) are antiseptic, carminative, warming; relieve muscle spasms and increase perspiration (warming). Tea stimulates bile secretion. Leaf and flower extraction are Commission E–approved in Germany for treating dyspepsia and gallbladder and liver problems.

PICKERELWEED
Pontederiaceae *(Pontederia cordata)*

Identification: Arrow-shaped leaf, veins spread from base, merge at tip like venation in grass leaves; blue flowers in densely clustered spikes.

Habitat: Ponds and lakes in entire United States except extreme desert, southern California, and lower Florida.

Food uses: Young leaves (before they emerge from the water), mature seeds, and leaves eaten. Leaves are most tender in spring, while unfurling beneath water. Cook leaves with dandelions and mustard greens. Season cooked greens with Italian dressing or herbes de Provence; serve hot. Add flower petals to salads. In late summer seeds mature in tough, leathery capsules. Open capsule to get fruit. Munch as a trail food, or dry and grind into flour.

Pickerelweed

Medicinal uses: Infusion of whole plant historically used by 2 North American native tribes as a contraceptive. See Daniel Moerman, *Native American Ethnobotany*.

REED GRASS
Poaceae *(Phragmites communis)*

Identification: Tall wetland grass; lance-shaped leaves up to 1' in length; flowers in tall, dense plume. Plants grow in dense cluster. Found around the margins of streams and in wet lowlands. The root of reed grass, like cattail roots, harvested and leached of its starch.

Reed grass

Habitat: Wetlands throughout the United States.

Food uses: The first shoots of spring are eaten raw but are best steamed until tender. I prefer to cut open the reed shoot to chew and suck the young shoots, then spit out the pulp. Prepare the plant immediately after picking, as delays in preparation make for a tough, stringy meal. Simply chop the new shoots into a manageable size and place them in a steamer. They are ready to eat in 5 minutes. In the fall, seeds ground into flour or stripped, crushed, and cooked with berries. Also try reed seeds cooked in stews and soups.

Medicinal uses: The Chinese use plant to clear fevers, quench thirst, and promote diuresis and salivation.

Note: The dried, hollow stalks of reed are cut to 4" lengths and used as spigots for tapping maple trees for syrup.

RICE, WILD
Poaceae *(Zizania aquatica, Z. palustris)*

Identification: Tall grass with a somewhat reedlike flower head; long, narrow leaf blades; flowers in tall plume; upper flowers female, lower flowers male.

Habitat: Wild rice found growing in shallow, clean, slow-moving water east of the Missouri River.

Wild rice

Food uses: Seeds harvested in August and September. Timing is critical, so check your stand of wild rice often. Mature seeds drop off easily. Return every other day to maximize the harvest. Use a rolling pin to thresh the husks from the seed. Simply roll back and forth over the grain. Use a fan or the wind to dispel the chaff. Cooking tips: The simplest way to cook wild rice is to boil 2 cups of lightly salted water, add 1 cup of wild rice, cover, and simmer for 35 minutes. Wild rice is an excellent stuffing for wild turkey. Wild rice, cooked until tender, is an excellent addition to pancake and waffle mixes. It also goes well in 12- and 20-grain hot cereals and is a great substitute for white rice. Extend your supply by cooking it with equal parts of long-grain brown rice.

Medicinal uses: Staple cereal crop for Native Americans, providing winter nutrition in a harsh climate.

SWAMP DOCK; CURLY DOCK
Polygonaceae *(Rumex orbiculatus, R. crispus, R. patientia)*

I include all docks here, although *R. crispus* and *R. orbiculatus* are typically found along the edges of roadsides, in gardens, and meadows.

Identification: The many varieties of dock are common weeds growing on disturbed ground, edges of fields, roadsides, and vacant lots. Leaves typically widest at base, narrow to tip, rounded at base; paperlike flower spikes. Fruits 3 parted, brownish to red; each mature ovary contains a nutlet. Docks emerge in the spring, first as unfurling leaves; later, the flower spike shoots up with smaller leaves attached. Flowers and eventually seeds cluster along the top several inches of the spikes. Swamp or water dock (*R. orbiculatus*) is found growing in water or along stream margins. It is stout and tall (to 6') with a long root and flat, narrow, dark green leaves. Both curly dock (*R. crispus*) and yellow dock (*R. patientia*) have curly or wavy leaf margins.

Habitat: Entire United States except arid areas, along streams, in marshes and wetlands.

> **WARNING: Contains oxalic acid; like spinach, do not eat more than twice a week.**

Food uses: My favorite species is *R. crispus*. It grows in profusion in the garden and is available as food in March. Leaves and seeds are edible; tender young leaves, as they emerge, are most edible. Older leaves are tough and bitter and must be cooked

Swamp dock

in 2 changes of water. Steam, sauté, or stir-fry young leaves; season with ginger, soy, lemon juice, and sesame seed oil. Leaves are great with walnuts and raisins. Dock seeds are edible in late summer and autumn. Hulled seeds can be ground into flour and used as a soup thickener or as a flour extender in baked goods.

Medicinal uses: Curly dock and yellow dock are used by naturopaths and mid-wives as a tea to treat anemia and raise

Curly dock

iron levels in pregnant women. Iron in this form does not cause constipation. Curly dock root also used with vinegar to treat ringworm. All dock roots are laxative, bitter digestive stimulants.

WATERCRESS
Brassicaceae *(Nasturtium officinale)*

Identification: Grows along the margins of shallow, clean water. Alternate leaves to ¾" wide, ovate, simple, broad near base; small white flower with 4 petals. Avoid contamination from pesticides and herbicides—collect watercress (for that matter, all edible water plants) from a clean water source such as a highland stream or free-flowing spring.

Habitat: Throughout the United States in springs and free-flowing streams with rich bottoms.

> **WARNING: It's a good idea to cook all watercress gathered from the bush to avoid possible contamination with giardia and other waterborne parasites and contaminants.**

Food uses: Watercress is a pungent, spicy green. It's an important ingredient in V8 vegetable juice and one of the most useful greens known to humankind. In the northern United States and Canada, watercress is available 10 months a year. South of the Mason-Dixon Line, it's a year-round food. Watercress is high in vitamins A and C. Scramble chopped watercress with eggs, stuff a pita sandwich, add it to salads, or make watercress soup. I like to stir-fry watercress with 1 table-

Watercress

spoon olive oil, 2 tablespoons soy sauce, 1 tablespoon lemon juice, 1 teaspoon diced gingerroot, and the juice of 1 pressed garlic clove; cook briefly at medium heat for about 2 minutes. Use watercress as a stuffing when preparing smoked or baked bass. After washing the body cavity, stuff the fish with watercress, season to taste, and bake or smoke it. I like watercress as a wild ingredient on pizza.

Medicinal uses: Mild diuretic. A few Native American groups used watercress to dissolve gallstones.

YELLOW POND LILY; SPATTERDOCK

Scrophulariaceae *(Nuphar variegatum, N. luteum)*

Identification: These 2 closely related species are found in ponds, shallow lakes, and streams. Their disk-shaped leaves unfurl above water. The yellow flower blooms through the summer and bears a primitive-looking fruit. The fruit pod contains numerous seeds—

Spatterdock

perhaps the only palatable part of this plant.

Habitat: Throughout the United States except extreme mountain and desert regions. The Yellowstone National Park variety (long isolated) is about one-third larger in size.

Food uses: The root stock of spatterdock is cut free and boiled. It smells sweet like an apple but is extremely bitter—even after cooking in 2 or 3 changes of water. Strictly a survival food; eat when nothing else is available. The seeds can be dried and ground into flour or prepared like popcorn. Place the dried seeds in a popcorn popper; cover the machine so the small seeds don't become airborne. The results are usually disappointing. Seeds simply pop open, but they're edible with salt and butter.

Medicinal uses: Root poultice over wounds, swellings, boils, and inflammations. Root tea.

Edible Plants of Eastern Forested Areas

CLEAVERS; BEDSTRAW
Rubiaceae *(Galium aparine)*

Identification: Weak, slender stem; 8 leaves in whorl; tiny white flowers. Found in woodlands, along streams, and in vacant lots, often around the roots of hardwoods and other trees. Mature plant clings to clothing.

Habitat: Hardwood forests in eastern United States, roughly to the Mississippi, north to Ontario, and south to Florida.

Food uses: Add young cleaver leaves to salads in early spring. Mature leaves are tough and must be boiled and sautéed. Seeds of summer can be roasted and ground into coffee substitute. It's better than chicory but far short of coffee.

Cleavers

Medicinal uses: Diuretic. Tea used for skin diseases such as psoriasis, seborrhea, and eczema. Whole plant juice taken internally for kidney stones and cancer.

FALSE SOLOMON'S SEAL
Liliaceae *(Smilacina* spp.)*

Identification: Solomon's seal has flower umbels in the notch of each leaf, whereas false Solomon's seal has a flower spike at the top of the plant. This is a perennial with adventitious root stocks that produce the solitary stem, with alternating, lance-shaped leaves, partially clasping the stem; white flowers in a cluster at the top of the plant.

Habitat: Western United States in coniferous forest areas to 8,000', and in the eastern hardwood forests and shaded dune areas along the Great Lakes, north to Ontario, south to Kentucky and Tennessee.

Food uses: The young shoots of false Solomon's seal are edible. Berries may be eaten when ripe; be careful of the large hard seed. Green young berries

False Solomon's seal

may be emetic (may cause you to vomit). Root stocks of false Solomon's seal are inedible unless precooked in lye to remove bitterness. Sample this plant judiciously. This is a beautiful herbal that needs little care and has a different look each season.

Medicinal uses: Buds infused to treat chronic conditions; little documentation available.

GINGER, WILD
Aristolochiaceae *(Asarum canadense)*

Identification: Aromatic root, smells like ginger; 2 dark green heart-shaped leaves; note the hairy stem and leaves; primitive flower emerging under the leaves in May in Michigan. Grows from a spreading, adventitious rhizome. Found on rich soil in moist woods as a spreading ground cover in shady areas.

Wild ginger

Habitat: Various species grow across the entire United States except extreme desert, southern California, and lower Florida.

Food uses: Crushed root added to salad dressings. When dried and grated, it is an adequate substitute for Oriental ginger. For the daring gourmet, try boiling the root until tender and then simmer in maple syrup. The result is an unusual candy treat. Taste the leaves.

Medicinal uses: Roots traditionally used to treat colds and cough; antiseptic and tonic. Herbalists use the root in tincture to dilate peripheral blood vessels; unproven.

GINSENG; DWARF GINSENG
Araliaceae *(Panax quinquefolius)*

Identification: Rare perennial. Straight, erect stem with 2 or 3 leaf stems; typically 5 but up to 11 leaves per stem. The best place to find ginseng is in cultivation or at a botanical garden. Plant protected in most states, but you can order roots from Pacific Botanicals (pacificbotanicals.com) and other purveyors.

Habitat: Eastern United States, roughly to the Mississippi River, in rich moist woods, well drained, in dark and dank places. The easier-to-find dwarf ginseng is more prevalent. Plant is cultivated in the East and West and readily available in various forms.

Ginseng

Dwarf ginseng

Food uses: American ginseng root, a prized medicinal in China, sells for about $300 per pound in markets there. Cook the root in chicken soup. Eat the berries. Dried root can be ground with an old-fashioned sausage grinder then simmered in water as a pick-me-up. Add root slices to gin, vodka, bourbon to extract the virtues—it relieves the pressures of life!

Medicinal uses: Ginseng root's active ingredients, called saponins (glycosides), raise blood pressure, others lower it; some raise blood sugar, some lower it. Saponins from ginseng show an anticancer chemotherapy in preliminary studies.

GREENBRIER
Smilacaceae *(Smilax rotundifolia)*

Identification: A climbing vine with short tough thorns, squarish stem. Leaves are alternate, glossy green, broad and roundish, heart-shaped, 2"–5" in width; clinging tendrils sprout from the leaf axils. Leaf veins radiate from a petiole, petioles conspicuous. Small, green-white flowers in the spring produce a blue-black berry from late summer that lasts until the spring.

Habitat: Greenbrier is widespread in forests and thickets from Florida to Ontario, to the west to include Texas and Oklahoma. Abundant in sandy, shady dunes areas around the Great Lakes, climbing through and above plants on the forest floor.

Greenbrier

Food uses: Greenbrier can be eaten like asparagus when young and tender. Eat leaves and tendrils. Native Americans crushed and dried shoots, leaves, and tendrils and then boiled them to make jelly. Flavor with honey or maple syrup. The same powder may be used as a thickening agent in soups and stews. Infusion of dried leave drinkable with a sweetener.

Medicinal uses: Vines and leaves are crushed, made into a water decoction, and taken internally to treat pain.

GROUNDNUT
Fabaceae *(Apios americana)*

Identification: Climbing, pealike vine; numerous tubers along length of root. Leaves alternate, compound, feather-like; seeds in long pods.

Habitat: Groundnut grows on wet ground, along the fringes of streams, bogs, and thickets, and climbing shrubs, twining its way toward the sun, in shoe-wetting and deeply shaded marshes.

Groundnut

Easily transferred to your garden, where the root can be harvested in the autumn or spring. Found across the entire United States except extreme desert, southern California, and lower Florida.

Food uses: Seeds are edible. Cook them like lentils. Tubers of *Apios* are 15 percent protein—a great potato substitute. Native Americans established settlements near this staple—a high-protein foraging food.

Medicinal uses: This is a case of your-food-is-your-medicine: Native Americans used the pealike, lentil-like seeds as survival food. Most eastern tribes ate the seeds and roots, without which they may have starved in the winter.

INDIAN CUCUMBER
Liliaceae *(Medeola virginiana)*

Indian cucumber

Identification: Ovate to lanceolate pointed leaves, typically 7 in a whorl around stem. Blue berries. Plant grows 5"–7" tall.

Habitat: Moist deciduous forest, found around the base of oaks. Favorite place is the back entrance to Grand Mere State Park, Stevensville, Michigan.

Food uses: Indian cucumber root has an edible root tuber—root tastes like cucumber—wash and eat raw. Gouge out of the ground with your fingers and eat fresh.

Medicinal uses: Whole plant infused and used externally on many skin ailments—considered a panacea by Native Americans. Berries used as an anticonvulsive. Dried leaves and berries given to youngsters and babies in infusion. Root tea also used as a diuretic to treat congestive heart failure.

JACK-IN-THE-PULPIT; INDIAN TURNIP
Araceae *(Arisaema triphyllum)*

Indian turnip

Identification: Leaves compound, 3 leaflets, oval, smooth, lighter underside; distinctive primitive flower, spadix in pulpit-like spathe.

Habitat: Found in rich soils, generally woods or shady lowland, with skunk cabbage and mayapple nearby. Found across the entire United States except extreme desert, southern California, and lower Florida.

Food uses: Native Americans sliced roots and dried them, deactivating calcium oxalate. Dried root was cooked twice (boiled and then sautéed) and eaten like potato chips. I consider this a survival food—eat to survive, not to thrive.

Medicinal uses: Plant parts used to treat cough, sore throat, ringworm, and as a poultice for boils and abscesses.

MARSH MARIGOLD; COWSLIP
Ranunculaceae *(Caltha palustris, Caltha* spp.*)*

Identification: Leaves ovate on yellow-green stems; distinctive fluorescent yellow flowers.

Habitat: Thrives in sunlight to partial shade. Plants grow in low wetlands, often in large colonies, in marshes, along stream edges and wet fields, often with roots submerged in water.

Marsh marigold

Found across the entire United States except extreme desert, southern California, and lower Florida.

Food uses: Leaves eaten as a potherb in the spring before the flowers open (cook twice, boil them, sauté, then do it all again). Cooking in several changes of water denatures the caustic alkaloid. Actually, leaves are extremely bitter and not worth the time and trouble. So why do I put it here? This lovely plant is worth your attention.

Medicinal uses: Leaves used as laxative and cough syrup. Root used in decoction for colds.

RAMPS; WILD LEEKS
Liliaceae *(Allium tricoccum)*

Identification: Strong onion aroma; long, wide leaves grow directly from bulb on short stem. Leaves are transient, gone from the plant in 3–4 weeks, giving rise to a flowering stem and white flowers. By July all that is evident of the plant is a stem with shiny black seeds. Bulb is still there, so dig.

Wild leeks

Habitat: Eastern United States, roughly to the Mississippi River. Found on banks in wet woods, above seeps, on rich and moist hillsides, deciduous forest, especially beech-maple climax woods.

Food uses: Leaves, stems, and bulbs are edible—marvelous in stews and soup, or sautéed with soy sauce, extra-virgin olive oil, and a little water to keep plants from sticking to pan. For a martini treat, stuff fresh bulbs in large olives, drop olives in the martini. Did I mention pizza? Delicious—and an absolute must in tomato sauce.

Medicinal uses: Used as a tonic to combat colds. Disputed evidence suggests eating raw bulbs may reduce risk of heart disease. Chop leaves into chicken soup to potentiate this cold and flu fighter.

RUE ANEMONE; WOOD ANEMONE; WINDFLOWER
Ranunculaceae *(Thalictrum thalictroides)*

Windflower

Identification: Windflower is a member of the buttercup family with small and delicate lobed leaves that shake in the lightest breeze, thus the common name. Perennial grows to 8", has a white flower with 6 petals; an early bloomer, typically April in Michigan; sooner in Kentucky and Tennessee. Root consists of 2–4 attached tubers.

Habitat: Found on the floor of hardwood forests of the East, in well-drained soil, scattered here and there over the ground.

> **WARNING: Potentially toxic; avoid this plant as a foodstuff. I include this plant here because of its extensive availability. You will find it and become curious, but don't eat it.**

Food uses: I have eaten these peppery roots in small quantities. Starchy root said to be edible after cooking, but most members of the buttercup family are toxic. Regardless of what other field guides may say, I recommend that you do not eat this root.

Medicinal uses: Cherokee used a tea of the root to stem diarrhea. Root tea was used to stem vomiting.

SOLOMON'S SEAL
Liliaceae *(Polygonatum biflorum)*

Identification: Rising from an adventitious root (where the previous year's growth leaves a seallike scar), a single stalk with lance-shaped leaves. The buds and flowers are in the notches (leaf axils) of the leaves. Flowers greenish-white, bell shaped, producing a blue-black berry.

Habitat: Hardwood forests from the East Coast to Nebraska, north to Ontario and south to Louisiana, Florida, and Texas.

Food uses: Starchy rhizomes used as food; must be cooked. Young shoots of Solomon's seal are fair as a trail food. Must be steamed, boiled, or cooked.

> **WARNING: Sample judiciously. Large quantities may be harmful. Berries considered poisonous. I have nibbled on a few and I'm still here (though some would say my mind is gone).**

Medicinal uses: Purchase sliced and dried roots of Chinese Solomon's seal in Chinese supermarkets. The root is rich in polysaccharides and considered antidiabetic. Cook the store-purchased Chinese variety in stir-fries or in noodle soups. *Polygonatum* root used by holistic practitioners and Native

Solomon's seal —45 years in my garden

Americans, sliced and infused in water to treat indigestion, excessive menstruation, and exhaustion. Cold wine root infusion used in Spanish medicine with arnica tincture to clear or prevent bruises.

SPRING BEAUTY; INDIAN POTATO; MOUNTAIN POTATO
Portulacaceae *(Claytonia caroliniana, C. lanceolata, C. tuberosa)*

Identification: Approximately 7" tall; narrow lance-shaped leaves die off after bloom; flowers ⅓" across, light pink to white or white with pink veins, in loose terminal clusters, numbering 3–18. Plant grows from ground, where it is attached to an acorn-size, fleshy corm (oval or globular stem base swollen with food and water surrounded by papery scale). Emerges and blooms in early spring.

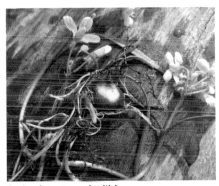

Spring beauty and edible corm

Habitat: Found in rich, moist woods throughout the East and across the United States and the Mountain West on wooded stream banks. Rare or not found in extreme desert, southern California, lower Florida, and the prairie states.

Food uses: The brown-skinned corm is edible. Peel the skin, wash, and eat raw or cooked. Try it on the grill with roasted vegetables. Roll the corm in olive oil, and then roast for about 8 minutes until browned. Flowers are edible but bland. Young leaves boiled for 10 minutes and eaten, but poor tasting. The real beauty of this plant is in the eyes of the beholder—as a foodstuff it's best left alone.

Medicinal uses: Tea from root used to reduce fever. Crushed leaves used as poultice over ulcers.

SWEET CICELY; WILD ANISE
Apiaceae (*Osmorhiza odorata*, other *Osmorhiza* spp.)

Identification: Perennial with slightly thickened roots, often in a cluster. Broken root smells like anise. Plant to 3' tall with bright green to greenish, shiny leaves; small greenish-white flowers in umbels (hemlock-like).

Sweet cicely

Habitat: Typically hardwood forest (shaded or partially shaded), often found around the base of trees; located in the entire United States except extreme desert, southern California, and lower Florida.

> **WARNING: Looks like poison hemlock. First-time foragers: Collect only with an expert. Find an expert at your county or state park who gives wild plant talks and walks.**

Food uses: Wild anise, commonly called sweet cicely, has a sweet anise odor and taste. Use as an anise substitute to spice cooked greens. Add leaves to salads.

Medicinal uses: Leaves occasionally eaten by diabetics as sugar substitute.

TOOTHWORT, CUT-LEAF
Brassicaceae (*Cardamine laciniata*)

Identification: Perennial to 6", with deeply cut leaflets, typically 5 lobed leaflets per leaf; 3 compound leaves in a whorl around plant. Flower blue-white to pinkish. Early spring bloomer, often in dense colonies.

Toothwort

Habitat: Hardwood forests of the East, from Ontario to Georgia, Maine to Iowa. Shade dwelling, typically found under oaks, beech, and maple. Blooms April–May.

Food uses: A favorite cooked green of the Cherokee, cut-leaf toothwort has an edible flower and edible root. I have not used this plant much. I like to munch on the flowers in the spring while fly-casting on Volinia Creek near Dowagiac, Michigan.

Medicinal uses: Root used to treat toothache. Chew the root. Root also chewed for colds, flu. A decoction or tea of the root is used to clear the throat of phlegm or as a gargle for treating sore throats. Root chew also reported to treat hoarseness. The chewed root placed as a poultice over the head and temples to treat headache.

TRILLIUM, WHITE
Liliaceae (*Trillium grandiflorum*)

Identification: Leaves, sepals, and flower petals in 3s. Blankets eastern woods in spring.

Habitat: Deciduous forest in East, shade to partial shade, typically in mature woods, such as a beech-maple climax forest. Various species found in entire United States except extreme desert, southern California, and lower Florida.

White trillium

Food uses: There are several varieties of trillium. The leaves and white, red, and purple flowers are edible, but for my taste, members of this genus are too pretty to eat. *Trillium* and toad-shade (a red-flowered species) are easy to grow in the home garden. Locate in shade and rich soil.

Toadshade

Medicinal uses: Native Americans used a root bark decoction of *T. grandiflorum* for ear sores; splinters of wood soaked in root extraction and then pricked through the skin over arthritic joints to relieve pain.

TROUT LILY
Liliaceae (*Erythronium americanum*)

Identification: Yellow-flowered trout lily has mottled, shiny leaves and a small, yellow, lily-like flower. Plant is 6"–8" tall, often sub-arboreal (around base of hardwoods in East) in colonies that may blanket the forest floor. Avalanche lilies of the Mountain West are close relatives with edible bulbs.

Trout lily

Habitat: Found on moist forest floor. Various species both east and west of the Mississippi River, from the East Coast to the coastal mountains of the West.

WARNING: Plant protected in many states.

Food uses: Young leaves boiled and sautéed, with unremarkable results. Tuber may be sliced and eaten after boiling.

Medicinal uses: Root infusion used to reduce fevers. Crushed leaves used as a moist poultice over wounds and irritations.

VIOLETS, WOODLAND

Violaceae *(Viola spp.)*

Violets are cultivated in France for perfume. This incredible edible is high in vitamins A, C, and E.

Identification: Flower irregular; leaves vary, usually ovate; common blue violet has heart-shaped, serrated leaves—a volunteer found in shady areas along fringes of lawn.

Violet

Habitat: Yellow and white-flowered violets as well as bird's-foot violets are found in eastern woods and montane areas of the West, coast-to-coast in forested areas, lowlands, and mountains. They prefer moist forests, conifers, or hardwoods.

> **WARNING: Late-season plants without flowers can be confused with inedible greens. Forage this plant only when in bloom.**

Food uses: Use both the leaves and flowers in salads. Flowers may be candied: Dissolve sugar in alcohol, brush on hypertonic solution, and let crystallize. Experiment! Put them over finished meat dishes as a garnish and color contrast that invite eating. I like plucking the flowers and munching them as I hike through the forest.

White violet

Medicinal uses: Violet roots consumed in large amounts are emetic and purgative. Plant used as poultice over skin abrasions. In China indigenous health-care givers use one species, *V. diffusa*, to treat aplastic anemia, leukemia, mastitis, mumps, and venomous snakebites. The violet's color suggests the presence of anthocyanin, a secondary metabolite that gives off a blue hue. Anthocyanin also provides protection from *E. coli* infection.

Trees and Nuts

ALDER
Betulaceae *(Alnus* spp.*)*

Alder

Identification: These members of the birch family grow to 80', but often much smaller. Bark smooth and gray when young, gets coarse and whitish-gray when mature. The bark on *Alnus rubra* turns red to orange when exposed to moisture. Leaves are bright green, oval, coarsely toothed, and pointed. Male flowers are clustered in long hanging catkins; female seed capsule is ovoid cone; seed nuts small, slightly winged, and flat.

Habitat: Alder prefers moist areas. Species range from California to Alaska east to Idaho. Numerous species found across North America, often in impenetrable mazes surrounding streambeds—great bear habitat; be careful.

Food uses: Members of this genus provide firewood in the Northwest for savory barbecue cooking. Smoking helps preserve meat. Soak meat in a salt brine, then smoke. The bark and wood chips are preferred over mesquite for smoking fish, especially salmon. Scrape sweet inner bark (in early spring) and eat raw, or combine with flour to make cakes.

Medicinal uses: Sweat-lodge floors were often covered with alder leaves, and switches of alder were used to apply water to the body and the hot rocks. Alder ashes used as a paste and applied with an alder chewing stick to clean teeth. Cones of subspecies *A. sinuata* used as medicine, as are other alder species. Spring catkins smashed to pulp and eaten as a cathartic (help move bowels). The bark mixed with other plants in decoction and used as a tonic. The decoction of the female catkins used to treat gonorrhea. A poultice of leaves applied to skin wounds and skin infections. In the Okanagan area of central Washington and British Columbia, First People used an infusion of new end shoots, new plant tops, as an appetite stimulant for children. Leaf tea infusion said to be an itch- and inflammation-relieving wash for insect bites and stings, poison ivy, and poison oak. Upper Tanana informants reported that a decoction of the inner bark reduces fever. Infusion of bark used to wash sores, cuts, and wounds. This is still an important "warrior plant" in sweat-lodge ceremonies, a cleansing spiritual rite.

Note: Smoking meat with alder: Wood chips are soaked overnight in water then placed on coals or charcoal to smoke meat. In 1961 I saw more than 100 Native Americans smoking fish, moose, and caribou for winter storage along a 10-mile stretch of the Denali Highway in Alaska. Local hunting rules at the time required any person who shot a caribou to give some of the meat to the First People, who preserved it for winter food. Fish flayed, stabbed through with a stick, and hung from wood weirs above a smoldering alder fire until smoked and dry. In hardwood-impoverished areas of the West, red alder burns slower than pine and is a suitable home-heating fuel. Bark may be stripped and soaked in water to make an orange to rust-colored dye.

BEECH TREE; AMERICAN BEECH
Fagaceae (Fagus grandifolia)

Beech

Identification: Tall (to 160') tree; leaves alternate, toothed, straight, and parallel veined, short stalked; bark light gray and smooth; twigs slender with long narrow scaly buds. Beechnut fruit (to ¾" long) is in a spiny husk, meat protected by a tough shell—fruits fall in late summer.

Habitat: Climax species in eastern forests. Beech and hard maple end the process of succession in hardwood forests. Prefers rich soil, open forest. Chemical in plant kills most understory competitors.

Food uses: Years ago hogs roamed the eastern forests eating the nuts. Quite a feat, as the nuts, encased in a durable husk, then a shell, leave little room for meat. Tasty though. Squirrels will get to the nuts before you can. Watch a squirrel in a beech forest—it may lead you to a cache of hundreds of nuts. Good luck.

Medicinal uses: Bark decoction taken to induce abortions; also used for pulmonary problems. Leaves decocted and compressed as a poultice over wounds and sores. Leaf decoction also used over burns. Nuts eaten to treat worms, much the same as pumpkin seeds.

BUTTERNUTS
Juglandaceae (Juglans cinerea)

Butternut

Identification: Grows to 120'; round top, smooth bark; young branches light gray, becoming light brown and deeply fissured. Buds dark brown, ovoid, and flattened; leaves to 25" long and shorter, with stout petioles, compound with 11–17 oblong lance-shaped leaflets, 2"–4" long; thick-husked fruit in clusters, nut elongated compared to a walnut.

Habitat: Southwestern Michigan stretches the northern limit of this eastern tree, from New Brunswick to Alabama, Virginia to South Dakota. Tolerates drier climates, but prefers rich, moist banks near streams and rivers.

Food uses: Biggest of the walnut family; spoils quickly. Collect butternuts from ground and throw them in water; those that sink are worth opening. Floating nuts have had an adventurous creature in them eating the nut meat. Native Americans crushed and ground nut meats to paste as a baby food.

Medicinal uses: Juglone—in the bark, root, and seed hulls—is anticancer, antimicrobial, cathartic, and antiparasitic. Native Americans used bark decoction to treat diarrhea and as a purgative; an infusion of buds to treat mouth sores, mouth ulcers, and to cleanse breath.

CHESTNUT
Fagaceae (*Castanea dentata*)

Chestnut

Identification: American chestnut, to 100', is round topped with horizontal limbs; mature branches dark brown, yellow-green when young. Leaves oblong to lance shaped, with short petioles, leaves shiny green turning yellow in the fall. Nut shell covered with numerous spines, opens with first frost to bear shelled nut. Chestnuts found in botanical gardens and secret hideaways. More common is the Chinese chestnut. Do not confuse these trees with the buckeye or horse chestnut. Chestnuts may be removed from their spiny husk, then crack the protecting shell and eat fresh whole, sliced, as a meal (ground), or roasted. Try them roasted in stuffing for goose, turkey, duck, or chicken.

Habitat: Throughout eastern United States, from Maine to Florida, east to Ontario and the Mississippi River. Prefers moist forest and thrives on a variety of soils.

Food uses: Native Americans dried then ground chestnuts and used the meal to make bread. I like it in gravies, stuffing, cooked in a soup. Try roasting the nuts, then grinding them and making coffee. Tamale masa made with ground chestnut and cornmeal—delicious. I like them mashed to meal, then mixed with dried currants and dried cranberries and cooked in my 7-grain hot cereal. Nut meats are delicious in potato soups, corn soups, and various chowders. Try them added to hominy or mixed in corn bread. Smash a few nuts and mix them in sweet potato soup or mashed potatoes.

COCONUT PALM; COCOS
Arecaceae (Cocos nucifera)

Identification: Ringed scars left by fallen palm leaf. Leaves 12'–20' long, pinnate; consisting of linear-lanceolate, more or less recurved, rigid, bright green leaflets. Flower arising at leaf axils and enveloped by a spathe. Flowers bear lance-shaped petals, 6 stamens, and an ovary consisting of 3 connate carpels. Fruit 2½–5 pounds in weight and as big as a human head.

Coconut

Habitat: Subtropical, abundant on coastal areas of Florida. The coconut palm thrives on sandy, saline soils; requires abundant sunlight and regular rainfall; often located just above the tidal zone along tropical and subtropical beaches—transplant to yards and gardens in same climate.

Food uses: Soft fresh endosperm (milk and soft meat) used to feed infants when mother's milk not available—often mixed with bananas. Hispanics mix corn water and soy milk with the coconut milk as a nutritious food for infants and children. Coconut milk said to prevent curdling of milk in infants. Coconut meat is nutritious and eaten raw, cooked, shredded, or sweetened.

Medicinal uses: Coconut oil used cosmetically on the skin as a moisturizer. Hawaiian people use this as a complete body lotion, excellent for massage. Inhaling smoke from burning the fruit shells said to induce abortion. Meat rubbed on the head as a brain tonic; dried ash of meat eaten as a tonic. Endosperm considered a good food for diabetics if unsweetened. In Mexican medicine, meat and milk thought useful for treating diarrhea, dysentery, colitis, gastritis, indigestion, ulcers, and hepatitis. Meat and endosperm milk considered a tonic, used to rehabilitate the physically weak. Oil is an effective moisturizer. Soft flesh rubbed on acne, wrinkles. Coconut milk taken with lime juice is a refrigerant (cooling); rehydrates children and adults; lowers acidity of urine.

HAZELNUT
Betulaceae (Corylus cornuta)

Identification: Tall shrubs or small trees with leaves to 5", coarse, toothed (double toothed). Nuts in a bristly husk. Often found as understory, rich soil preferred, along edges of woods, fens, and marshes.

Habitat: Beaked hazelnut is abundant in southern Michigan and Washington State—where it is cultivated. Wild

Hazelnut

strains found here and there and in between.

Food uses: You have to beat the squirrels to these, favorite nut of the fox squirrel. Remove husk, roast, and eat. Not bad raw. Nuts can be ground into nut flour; great nutritional boost to bread, pancakes, and waffles. Try cooking nuts in soups and stews and with game. Hazelnut bread is popular in Washington. Nuts dipped in honey and roasted—messy and delicious.

Beaked hazelnut

Medicinal uses: Native Americans infused branches and leaves to treat intestinal disorders and heart trouble. Boiled bark used to induce emesis.

HICKORY, SHAGBARK AND PIGNUT
Juglandaceae *(Carya ovata, C. glabra)*

Identification: Shagbark is a tree, 60'–90', with 5–7 hairless leaflets; compound leaves 8"–14" in length. Light-colored shedding bark indicative, often peeling (shagging) away from tree in long, narrow strips. Buds covered with overlapping scales. Nuts egg shaped in thick yellow husk splitting to base.

Hickory

Pignut hickory has alternate, compound leaves that are pinnate, 8"–10" long with 5–7 leaflets that are lance shaped and finely toothed; leaf stem is smooth. Bark of pignut is smooth compared to shagbark. Tree may grow to 100'. Flowers of both species are monoecious—males are yellow green drooping catkins, with 3 hanging from 1 stalk, 2"–3" long; females are very short and found in clusters at the end of the branches; both appear in spring. Shagbark species is more desirable the larger and more attainable nut.

Habitat: In deciduous forests of East, north to the Upper Peninsula of Michigan, south to the Gulf Coast states excluding Florida, west to the plains, and east to the coast.

Food uses: Tree tapped for sap; makes a unique and savory syrup with the flavor of hickory nuts. Nuts are edible and splendid—sweet and succulent, only surpassed by butternut. Use in salads, syrups, on pancakes and waffles, and everywhere a superior nut flavor is desired.

Note: Husking and shelling nuts is difficult work but worth the effort. I purchase mine (shelled) from an Amish family for about $8 a pint. I cannot do it that cheap.

Medicinal uses: Small shoots of spring steamed as a respiratory inhalant for congestion and headaches. Spring shoots placed on hot stones in sweat lodges for soothing inhalant. Bark boiled and decoction sipped to treat arthritis—this hot bark infusion considered a panacea, treatment for general malaise as a tonic.

LARCH; TAMARACK
Pinaceae (*Larix laricina*)

Larch

Identification: Medium to large wetlands tree of the North; at first appearance it looks like a typical pine or fir, needles slender to 1" in length emanating from short spurs on branch, in clusters, single or several, with non-drooping branch (European larch has drooping branches). Cones less than ¾" in length, almost round; bark flakes off in scales. Unlike pine and fir, larch is deciduous and loses its needles through the winter.

Habitat: Wetlands of the North, West, and Northwest, and along stream banks—prevalent along the South Shore Trail of Hyalite Reservoir in Montana. Bald cypress, a similar species, found in wet areas of the southern United States.

Food uses: Tender new shoots infused into tea or panfried as food. The inner bark can be scraped, dried, and pounded into flour; reconstitute with water and make flatbread.

Medicinal uses: Native Americans used the bark extraction and balsam (resin) of the plant in combination with other plants in decoction to treat acute infections such as colds, flu, fever, coughs. Various tribes utilized the bark infusion of young shoots as a laxative. Bark and wood poultice used to treat wounds and draw out infection. Inner bark infusion considered warming. The resinous balsam used as a stimulating inhalant. Leaves and bark were pounded, crushed, and used as a poultice to reduce headache. This ritual sweat-lodge plant is useful for relieving tension, backache, and headache. Needles, twig, bark wetted and applied to hot stones to produce steam. Western larch, *L. occidentalis*, found west of the plains states, is used in similar ways, including decoction of the new growth as a wash for cancer. The resinous pitch of the western species mixed with animal fat and used on wounds, cuts, and burns. *L. decidua*, tamarack's European cousin, is Commission E–approved for treating coughs, colds, bronchitis, and fever, and to promote resistance to acute infections.

Note: This rot-resistant relative of cypress is used to make long-lived railroad ties. The tree's tough, fibrous, and rot-resistant roots make good sewing and basket-weaving material and were often used to sew birch bark together to make canoes. Shredded inner bark fed to horses.

MADRONE
Ericaceae *(Arbutus menziesii)*

Madrone

Identification: Evergreen, broadleaf tree growing along the seacoast of the Northwest. Young bark is chartreuse and smooth, whole. Older bark is dark brown to red and peeling. Evergreen leaves are alternate, oval, 7" long, shiny, dark green above, lighter, whitish-green beneath, hairless, and leathery. White flowers that are urn shaped to 3" long in large drooping clusters. Fruit an orange-red berry about ½" across with a granular skin.

Habitat: Typically found in coastal areas of northern California, Oregon, offshore islands of Washington and British Columbia, in typically dry, sunny areas with a sea exposure.

Food uses: Vancouver Salish used reddish bark in decoction when cooking to dye edible camas bulbs pink. Berries cooked before eating; also stored after steaming, dried, and reconstituted in hot water before eating. Berries smashed and made into a cider-like drink. Cider claimed by Miwok as an appetite stimulant and said to resolve upset stomach. Berries are also dried and stored for later use.

Medicinal uses: Saanich and other nations used bark and leaves for treating colds, tuberculosis, stomach problems, and as a postpartum contraceptive. Decoctions of plant were also used as an emetic (Concow nation), which belays one from imbibing nonchalantly. Leaves used by Cowichan of Northwest as a burn treatment, dressing. Leaf infusion used to treat stomach ulcers. Also, fresh leaves eaten off tree for relieving cramps. Chewed leaves said to relieve sore throat (chew, swallow juice, but don't swallow leaves). Leaf infusion used by Skokomish to treat colds and ulcers. Bark infusion used to treat diarrhea. Bark decoction used for washing sores, wounds, impetigo; said to be astringent. Bark decoction also used as a gargle for sore throat, according to Pomo and Kashaya. Karok used leaves in puberty ceremony.

Note: The wood was used to make canoes, and the berries are used as steelhead trout bait. Berries also dried and used as beads for making bracelets and necklaces.

MAPLE, SUGAR
Aceraceae *(Acer saccharum)*

Identification: Leaves have the basic form of Canada's national emblem. Crowns of trees are broad and rounded in the open. Bark is smooth when young and furrows with age. Leaves are typically 3 lobed. Seeds have the characteristic helicopter-blade appearance and fly accordingly.

Habitat: Found in the eastern United States, Midwest, south-central and eastern Canada.

Food uses: The seeds are eaten but are poor tasting. Pluck the seeds from the helicopter-blade husk and cook like peas, or stir-fry. You will soon have your fill of them. Maple sugar and maple syrup from the winter and spring sap are what these trees are all about. A maple sugar mill near you has taps or information as to where to purchase them (they'll probably sell or give you a few). Use a brace and ⅜" bit to drill through the bark until you hit the hard-

Maple

wood. Clean the hole thoroughly, and then use a hammer to drive in the tap. Sap flows best on warm, sunny days after a freezing night. Tapping begins in late January and continues until the sap runs dark, thick, and stingy, in early April. With trees under 10" wide, use only 1 tap; for larger trees, drive 2 or 3 taps in a circle around the tree. Use a covered pail to collect the sap. If you are going to boil the sap down on an open fire, make certain your wood is dry and presents very little smoke. Smoke will impart an undesirable flavor to the syrup. I use 3 pans over a long and narrow firepit. I pour the sugar water from pan to pan as it cooks. Pan number 1 receives the fresh water from the trees, pan 2 will receive the reduced water from pan 1, and pan 3 receives the further-reduced water from pan 2. Pan 3 of course will have the thickest, richest water. Boil the syrup in pan 3 until it coats a spoon.

Medicinal uses: Maple syrup is a glucose-rich sugar substitute with the added benefit of numerous minerals. I prefer it as a sweetener rather than refined sugar, which has no minerals. Traditionally, maple syrup was used to flavor and sweeten cough syrups. The unfinished fresh sap is considered a mineral-rich tonic. I store a couple gallons in the freezer and keep one in the refrigerator as a flavorful and nutritious water source.

Note: Other trees tapped for sap include black walnut; white, black, and yellow birch; bigleaf maple. Grapevines can be cut (to save the tree) in the spring and provide copious amounts of mineral-laden water.

MAPLE, BIGLEAF AND OREGON BROAD-LEAF
Aceraceae (Acer macrophyllum)

Bigleaf maple

Identification: Large maple with large leaves, bark often entirely covered with moss when mature. May reach 120' in height. The young tree has smooth, green bark, maturing to gray-brown with ridges. Leaves are opposite, 5 lobed, 6"–12" wide. Leaves are dark green above and paler underneath;

leaf stalk may exude milky substance when broken or picked. Flowers are greenish-yellow, small in cylindrical clusters, and appear before leaves unfold. Seeds are paired and winged.

Habitat: Found in conjunction with Douglas fir, in dry to wet environments (Northwest rain forests), often in recently cleared areas, middle to low altitudes.

Food uses: Bark may be tapped for sugary water that is thickened by heat to make maple syrup. Freshly sprouted seeds are edible (get them early, they may grow 3' in 1 year). Use early flowers stir-fried or to garnish salads.

Medicinal uses: Sore throat relief.

Note: Use a ⅜ths drill bit and a standard metal tap. Drill ¾"–1" into and through bark; drive tap halfway and hang covered container from the tap. A 1" plastic pipe also works but requires a larger hole. Sap flows best in late winter (February) on sunny days. Steam off water to thicken at 170°F–180°F. Wood used by First People to make canoe paddles.

OAKS
Fagaceae *(Quercus* spp.*)*

Identification: This is a large genus with species worldwide. I prefer the acorns from oaks that have rounded instead of pointed leaf lobes. White oak (*Quercus alba*) and bur oak are good examples from the eastern United States. Chinkapin oak also has sweet acorns. *Q. alba* has white-gray bark; evenly lobed hairless leaves 3"–9" (7–11 lobes, not pointed) and twigs that are also hairless. Acorn cup (cap) is bowl shaped, covering one-third or less of acorn. Bur oak (*Q. macrocarpa*) is a tall tree (to 180') with leaves marked by deep indentations (1 or 2), dividing the leaves into 2 or more proportions. Leaves leathery and shiny above, hairy and whitish underneath. Acorn cups bowl shaped, with mossy (bur) fringe of elongated scales. Bark light gray, shallow grooved. Leaves 4"–10".

Bur oak

Habitat: Varieties of oaks are found throughout the United States: eastern forests, montane areas, California, Texas, New Mexico, Washington State. Bur oak, white oak, black oak, chinkapin, and red oaks are distributed throughout forests of the eastern United States.

Food uses: Oaks with leaves that are pointed have more tannins, and the acorns are too bitter to consume even after soaking in water. The best way to get acquainted with oaks and learn how to identify them is to visit an arboretum where oaks are labeled and identification is facilitated. Armed with this visual proof, you will be successful gathering nuts for the winter. White oak and bur oak have sweet nut meat. Tannins in acorn meat embitter the taste. Tannins are water-soluble phenolic compounds that leach away in water; thus a water bath sweetens the nut. A quick fix in the kitchen is to puree the acorn meat in water. Use a blender and combine 1 cup water with every cup of nut meat. Blend thoroughly. Press the water out of the nut meat through a clean pair of pantyhose, cheesecloth, or a clean white sock (a dirty white sock imparts an objectionable flavor to the nut meats). I like the acorn puree on baked potatoes, over tomato sauce, in all baking recipes, or to snack out of hand.

Medicinal uses: White oak has tannin-rich bark. Tannins are antiseptic and astringent. Native Americans and pioneers made a tea from the bark for mouth sores, burns, cuts, and scrapes. The bark considered by many a panacea. Tannins in oak and tea may provide cancer protection and are now under investigation. Native Americans used bark tea for treating fevers and hives. Bark tea is astringent.

Chinkapin oak

PECAN
Juglandaceae (*Carya illinoinensis*)

Identification: Leaflets 9–17 per leaf. End buds to 1" long with 2 or 3 pairs of nonoverlapping yellow hairy bud scales; twigs hairless, bark closely ridged and non-peeling. Hybrids have much bigger nut meats than wild types and grow to 160' in height. Nuts longer than wide, edible.

Pecan

Habitat: This fertile-soil, bottomland dweller where temperatures are moderate and there is ample humidity, may not bear fruit for 20 years. Typically found wild along the Mississippi River, more on the west side.

Food uses: I use pecans in salads, Paleo waffles, pancakes, cookies, candy, and with ham and vegetable dishes. The nut was stored for winter use. Make pesto with pecans instead of pine nuts.

Medicinal uses: Kiowa used a decoction of the bark to treat tuberculosis. Leaves crushed and rubbed over ringworm.

WHITE PINE; PINYON PINE
Pinaceae *(Pinus strobus, P. edulis)*

Identification: White pine grows to over 100' and displays 5 needles in clusters, typically each with a white stripe on the side of each needle; needles are 3 sided, 2½"–5" long. Branches form a whorl around trunk, and the age of the tree is determined by the number of whorls. Pine cones are elongated with flexible scales. Pinyon pine grows to 20', with brown cones, typically in pairs, that are 2"–4" long. Seeds are up to ½" in length, inside a shell.

White pine

Pinyon pine

Habitat: Because of its utility, white pine is found throughout the East and as an ornamental in many western states. Pinyon pine prefers a drier climate and grows at higher altitudes in the Mountain West—especially prevalent in the Four Corners area.

Food uses: White pine needles are made into tea: Take a handful of needles, crush them, and add them to a gallon jar of water containing mountain mint, lemon thyme, and lemon balm; squeeze in juice of ½ lemon and infuse in refrigerator for 6 hours. Uplifting! Seeds from both white and pinyon pine are eaten. Pinyon pine is the premier edible seed (pine nuts) and is mashed to a paste and mixed with berries and spices for an unusual candy treat. Seeds on all pines are edible, but many are too small to gather effectively.

Medicinal uses: Pine pitch used to seal wounds; it is antiseptic and disinfectant.

REDBUD TREE
Leguminosae *(Cercis canadensis)*

Identification: Small tree to 30', broad, open, and flat or rounded crown. Bark thin and gray on young stems; on older trees bark darkens to reddish-brown to black, forming lone narrow scaly ridges; inner bark red. Leaves alternate, simple, heart shaped, dark green above and paler beneath. Flowers April–May; irregular, light rose–colored, pealike flowers blooming before leaves open.

Redbud

Habitat: Southwestern Michigan and south, through the southern states. Understory tree of forests and stream borders in moist ground. Associated with elm, basswood, silver maple, red ash, mulberry, and hackberry. Shade tolerant.

Edible redbud blossoms

Food uses: I eat the flowers in spring and, a little later, the young fruiting bodies. The flowers are tart and go well in salads, pancakes, fruit dishes. The pods (a fruiting legume) are best when dipped in a batter and cooked tempura-style.

Medicinal uses: Native Americans used the inner bark and root for respiratory congestion, pulmonary congestion, whooping cough. According to James Duke in his *Handbook of Northeastern Indian Medicinal Plants*, the Delaware nation used the inner bark infusion to prevent vomiting and to reduce fevers.

SASSAFRAS
Lauraceae *(Sassafras albidum)*

Identification: Small to medium tree with mitten-shaped leaves (and other diverse shapes), aromatic leaves and twigs. The root is fragrant and smells a bit like root beer. Flowers are yellow-green.

Habitat: Found in eastern forests, often along the edges of woods and roadsides. It is a first growth in oak-hickory forests.

Sassafras

Food uses: Dried leaves of spring used as filé in gumbo. Crush the dried leaves of spring to powder and use as a spice. Also, spread the leaf powder on pasta, soup, cheese, and other savory dishes. For root tea, peel the root before you boil it.

Medicinal uses: Bark decoction used as a stimulant, pain reliever, astringent, and folk treatment for rheumatism. Safrole (found in leaves, roots, and bark) is touted to have a wide variety of medicinal uses, including treatment of scurvy, skin sores, kidney problems, toothaches, rheumatism, swelling, menstrual disorders, sexually transmitted diseases, bronchitis, hypertension, and dysentery.

> ***WARNING:** The root oil was used as an antiseptic until 1960, when the USDA declared it unsafe because of the content of safrole, a carcinogenic toxin. There are no proven effects as a medicine, and because of the toxic effects of safrole, the plant extracts should not be eaten. That said, I chew the end twigs for flavor.*

Note: When camping, use twigs as a toothbrush (chew stick). Chew the end of the twig until it is bristly, and then use the bristles to clean between your teeth. Extracts are used to make perfume and root beer.

WALNUT, BLACK
Juglandaceae *(Juglans nigra)*

Black walnut

Identification: Tree 50'–90' in height and 2'–3' in diameter with a straight, clear trunk and narrow crown. Twigs and branches are thick. Leaves alternate, pinnately compound, 12"–24" long, with 10–24 sharply oval, finely toothed, long-pointed leaflets 3"–3½" long; bright, clear yellow in autumn. Flowers are yellow-green; males in catkins 2½"–5½" long; females on short spikes near twig ends. Fruit round, 2"–2½" across, with a thick, green, non-splitting husk; nut inside is furrowed and hard; matures in late summer to fall.

Habitat: Deep, well-drained soils; grows best in rich bottomlands, moist coves, and streamsides; grows best on the lower north- or east-facing slopes.

Food uses: In baked goods, cereals, waffles, pancakes, salads. Or eat it on the hoof out of hand. This is a daily requirement in morning oatmeal. Try crushed black walnuts mixed in maple syrup.

Note: To remove the husk (stain-producing covering of the walnut), you may put nuts on a paved driveway and roll them under your shoe. Or jack up a car slightly (about 1") off the ground, engage the transmission, and let the walnuts shoot under the tire. Some people wear gloves and use a hammer to pound and tug the husk away. Before shelling, drop unshelled walnuts in a bucket of water—those that float have worms that have eaten the nut meat. Open only the ones that sink.

Medicinal uses: A cholesterol-reducing study in 1995 at Loma Linda University found participants who ate 20 percent of their daily calories from walnuts lowered their LDL ("bad" cholesterol) by 12 percent. More recent research in 2021 published in *Circulation* showed a half cup of walnuts per day lowered LDL and total cholesterol in participants. Walnuts may help prevent hyperthyroidism, scabies, may lessen inflammation of psoriasis and arthritis. Walnuts are rich in serotonin, mood-enhancing chemistry, and may improve satiety by reducing cravings, thereby treating obesity. Black walnut husk extract is antifungal. An antifungal compound: equal parts of tincture of goldenseal, cinnamon, tea tree oil, and black walnut husk tincture.

Edible Plants of the Mountain West

Note: Many of the desert, prairie, and wetland plants in this guide are also found in the West.

ARROW-LEAFED BALSAMROOT
Asteraceae *(Balsamorhiza* spp.*)*

Identification: Found in clumps and colonies, these plants have arrow-shaped, basal leaves, 8"–12" in length. Leaves are hairy, rough to the touch. Flowers are yellow and long stalked. Up to 22 yellow rays encircle the yellow disk of florets.

Balsamroot

Habitat: Grows on dry, stony slopes in the foothills and higher elevations of the Rockies from Colorado to British Columbia, widespread in the Bitterroots and other Idaho wilderness areas. Find balsamroot on the hike from Pebble Creek Campground in Yellowstone to the confluence of the Lamar River and Cache Creek (take along your fly rod).

Food uses: Young leaves and shoots are edible, as well as young flower stalks and young stems. They may be steamed or eaten raw. Peeled roots eaten, but taste bitter unless slow cooked to break down the indigestible polysaccharide (inulin). Roots may be cooked and dried, then reconstituted in simmering water before eating. Eat seeds out of hand or pounded into meal and used as flour. The roasted seeds can be ground into pinole. The Nez Percé roasted and ground the seeds, which they then formed into little balls by adding grease. In a pinch (should you get lost in these vast mountainous expanses), here is a readily available survival food, but freeing the root—often deeply and intricately woven into the rock—is an exhausting task.

Medicinal uses: Native Americans used the wet leaves as a wound dressing and a poultice over burns. The sticky sap was used to seal wounds and considered anti-septic. Balsamroot, when peeled and chewed, although bitter, contains inulin that may stimulate the immune system, providing protection from acute sickness, such as colds and flu. The sap is considered antibacterial and antifungal. A decoction of the leaves, stems, and roots administered for stomachache, colds. Root traditionally used for treating gonorrhea and syphilis. In sweat lodges, balsamroot smoke and steam said to relieve headaches. Considered a warrior plant in smudging ceremonies and a disinfectant; the inhaled smoke was said to relieve body aches. Chewed root used as a poultice over sores, wounds, and burns. Whole plant decocted for stomach pain.

AVALANCHE LILY; YELLOW AVALANCHE LILY
Liliaceae *(Erythronium grandiflorum, other Erythronium spp.)*

Identification: Leaves lance and ellipse shaped, narrowing at base, with a deeply buried, edible corm. Single yellow flower (sometimes 2) on 7"–8" stem (blooms in June and July).

Avalanche lily

Habitat: Found in alpine meadows and high slopes in western mountains. These species are similar to, and from the same genus as, the trout lily (dogtooth violet) of the eastern United States but are more sun tolerant.

Food uses: Reaching the corm is a difficult dig, requiring much effort. Native Americans wrapped the bulbs in cattails and reeds, then cooked them in an earth-filled pit over which a fire was burned; 10–12 hours in the pit would render the corms both edible and delicious.

> **WARNING: The corm contains the polysaccharide inulin—cook to make digestible. Plant protected in most areas.**

Medicinal uses: The inulin-rich bulb may be therapeutic to diabetics. (In Japan the inulin in burdock root is used to treat diabetics.)

BEAR GRASS; TURKEY BEARD; ELK GRASS
Liliaceae *(Xerophyllum tenax)*

Identification: Grasslike member of the lily family that grows as a clump of wiry, elongated, sharply pointed, saw-toothed blades to 2' in height. As it matures, an unbranched central stalk emerges, producing a terminal raceme (pyramidal cluster) of white flowers. Often found in groups, with several plants emanating from a single elongated rhizome, the plant produces 1 cluster of flowers before dying back.

Bear grass

Habitat: Found on mountain slopes to the timberline, from Alaska south to northern California. I have seen ample amounts near tree line on Mount Rainier, en route to the Burroughs at Sunrise, the northwest entrance to the park.

Food uses: Roots may be gathered and boiled or roasted until tender. Although not delicious, and for some not even good, it may provide the psychological lift one needs in a survival situation.

Note: Fragile bear grass is a barometer of ecosystem quality, and it is vanishing from numerous habitats—use only as a survival food. Florists gather leaves as filler for bouquets.

Medicinal uses: Native Americans chewed the roots and applied them as a poultice over wounds. Claimed to be hemostatic (stops bleeding). Roots chopped fine and prepared in decoction to treat broken bones and sprains. Roots have saponins, surfactant wetting agents that are used as a lather over wounds. For further reference, see Daniel Moerman's *Native American Ethnobotany*.

MEADOW BISTORT; ALPINE BISTORT; LADY'S THUMB
Polygonaceae (*Polygonum bistortoides, P. viviparum, P. persicaria*)

Bistort

Identification: Erect herb to 30", with lance-shaped basal leaves, flowers on erect stalk, producing brownish achenes (seeds). Flowers white in single dense cluster atop stalk, later forming a seed head.

Habitat: *P. bistortoides* and *P. viviparum* grow on wet, open slopes; abundant in the alpine meadows of Mount Rainier, the Cascades, from New Mexico to Alaska. South of Bozeman, Montana, on the Mirror Lake Trail, bistort spreads in abundance. Around 6 p.m. have your fly rod handy as the grayling feed on the surface for a furious hour of catch-and-release fishing. *P. persicaria* is found both east and west of the Mississippi in drier areas:, including vacant lots, meadows, and wet areas, including my garden.

Note: Easily identified and harvested in areas where harvesting is allowed.

Food uses: Young leaves and shoots edible raw or sautéed in butter; slightly sour taste—older leaves tough and stringy. Leaves in salads and cooked with meat. Starchy root is edible, boiled in soups and stews or soaked in water, dried and pounded (ground) into flour for biscuits, rolls, bread. Cooked roots said to taste like almonds, chestnuts. Seeds are edible and pleasant tasting.

Medicinal uses: Vitamin C–rich plant used to treat or prevent scurvy. Alcohol tincture is astringent and used externally on cuts, abrasions, pimples, insect stings and bites, inflammation, and infections. Little used today as a medicinal. Traditional uses still employed by montane-dwelling Native Americans and Europeans.

BLUEBELLS; CHIMING BELLS
Boraginaceae *(Mertensia spp.)*

Identification: Numerous species bear numerous blue (sometimes pinkish-blue) bell-shaped flowers (1" in length), that droop and, in a generous wind, appear to be ringing. Petals are fused. Succulent lance-shaped leaves are alternate, climbing the sturdy stem, and, as they approach the cluster of flowers, appear to be almost opposite. Plants spread in profuse colonies.

Chiming bells

Habitat: Taller species prefer moist meadows and stream banks, shorelines, seeps. Smaller subalpine and alpine species tolerate drier conditions. Meadows of chiming bells dominate the wet areas of East Ten Sleep Creek in the Bighorns of Wyoming.

Food uses: Leaves have an unusual and palatable flavor raw, steamed, or sautéed. Eat in moderation—the plant concentrates minerals, both good and bad.

Medicinal uses: Tea of aerial parts infused and taken to increase lactation. Infusion of leaves also used to treat symptoms of smallpox and measles.

BOG ORCHID, WHITE
Orchidaceae *(Platanthera dilatata)*

Identification: Frequently found in wet alpine meadows to 8,000'. Fleshy, thin-rooted perennial that may have tuber-like growths on roots. Plant grows to 35" tall but is typically shorter. Hairless and leafy stem. Leaves are lance shaped, blunt tipped or pointed, and get smaller as they rise up the stem. Upper leaves sheath leaves below and become more pointed as they climb the stem. Leaves are alternate, and lower leaves are up to 10" long and 1" wide. Flowers are white and somewhat green tinged, fragrant, and numerous on a tall green spike. Sepals are small, lance shaped; upper sepal is egg shaped, erect, and forms a hood. Flower comes directly from a bract, and petals are 1 or 2 veined; there is a nectar spur, and petals are slightly shorter and wider than sepals. Fruits (seeds) are erect, small, and elliptical.

Bog orchid

Habitat: Widespread in the western mountains, upper Midwest, Northeast states, and west to Oregon, Washington, and California. Not found in dry areas of the Southwest and southern Gulf Coast states. Found in wetlands, seeps, tundra, and stream banks, fens, bogs, and marshes. Prefers its roots in the water.

Food uses: Edible root is an emergency survival food that should be cooked. At best the root is bland; a few say it tastes like precooked frozen potatoes. Huh? Leaves are inedible, a few say toxic.

Medicinal uses: Plant is a traditional treatment for gravel (the production and movement of small stones from the kidneys to the bladder and then out of the body in urine).

Note: I call this an emergency survival food, as it is a beautiful and not-abundant orchid. Overharvesting could threaten its indigenous population. The taste is not worth the risk and mess of harvesting. Scented flower is exquisite.

DEVIL'S CLUB
Araliaceae *(Oplopanax horridus)*

Identification: Shrubby perennial to 10', a twisted tangle of spiny thorns. Has a sweet odor and displays large maplelike leaves armed on the underside with thorns. White flowers grouped in a club-like terminal head.

Habitat: Western mountains to the West Coast, especially in wet areas: seeps, stream banks, moist, low-lying forests—prevalent in the Olympic Range and Cascades, from sea level to tree line in Canada.

Devil's club

Food uses: Berries inedible, but spring buds eaten as a survival food (meaning in hard times, when people eat dirt). Pick young shoots with soft spines; get there early, right after the snow clears, before this armored plant walls itself off.

Medicinal uses: One of the most important medicinal plants of the West; roots, berries, and greenish bark are used. Berries rubbed in hair to kill lice and create a shine. Inner bark chewed raw as a purgative; decocted and imbibed for the same reason. Infused inner bark taken to relieve bowel and stomach cramps, arthritis, and ulcers. For further reference see the author's *Medicinal Plants of North America*.

ELK THISTLE
Asteraceae *(Cirsium scariosum)*

Identification: Spiny leaves in whorls around stem. Stem single spike or stem studded with spines and spiny leaves. Purple flowers are borne on the apex of the stem, flowers to 1½" wide.

Habitat: This thistle is abundant in meadows, subalpine and alpine lowlands in the Mountain West, especially

Elk thistle

abundant around Yellowstone. Found in Wyoming, Montana, Idaho, Washington, Colorado.

Food uses: Roots of elk thistle (also called meadow thistle) may be eaten raw, roasted, fried, pit-baked. Native Americans pit-baked the root. Cut this plant where it stands, slice away spines and skin, and eat the core like celery.

Medicinal uses: Roots of this thistle and others used as a poultice over wounds, swellings. Root decoction used for many purposes to include treating back pain. Whole plant smudged for treating headaches.

FIREWEED
Onagraceae (*Epilobium angustifolium, E. latifolia*)

Fireweed

Identification: Tall stem with narrow lance-shaped leaves that alternate, rising to a spire of pink flowers. Found singly or in colonies in burned-out areas, on disturbed ground, and along roadsides of the West. Erect stem bears a spired cluster of flowers with 4 petals. Leaf veins form loops that are distinctive; leaves paler underneath, darker on top. Seedpods borne on spire, mature, and release airborne fluffy seeds. Blooms April–August, depending on altitude.

Habitat: Burnouts, roadsides, disturbed areas in profusion, more sparsely elsewhere. Tolerates damp and dry areas, lowlands and highlands; some shade, but prefers drier areas, full sun.

Food uses: Edible flower, raw or cooked. Vitamin-rich leaves and tender shoots of early growth are steamed, sautéed, or stir-fried. Add tender young leaves to salads. Shoots pushing up from the ground are tasty, tender, and worth discovering.

Medicinal uses: Intense infusion of whole plant used as a laxative. Leaf and flower tea considered antispasmodic. Root chewed and used as a poultice over wounds. Whole-herb tea used to treat candidiasis.

GERANIUM
Geraniaceae (*Geranium viscosissimum,* other *Geranium* spp.)

Identification: Showy flowers with 5 petals from pale white to pink and purple. Plant grows to 3' but is usually smaller, in colonies, mixed with other wildflowers. Leaves are deeply cut, palmate, and plentiful. Plant blooms April–July, even into August at higher altitudes.

Habitat: Meadow varieties, alpine dwellers, and subalpine relatives near water sources in abundance at West Tensleep Lake Campground in the Bighorns off US 16 and Hyalite Canyon around Mirror Lake. Found in wet areas, grasslands, and around ponds and seeps.

Food uses: Sauté, or eat the flowers raw on the hoof. I avoid leaves, as they are more astringent, but when astringency is desirable, use prudently. Although not a favorite, this flower is abundant and can make the difference in a survival scenario.

Medicinal uses: Root decoction said to stem diarrhea. Leaf infusion, cooled and used as a gargle. Decoctions of the aerial parts of the plant used by several Native American tribes as a "life medicine"—a panacea, if you will—to treat internal ailments. Dried leaves used as a snuff to stem nosebleeds.

Geranium

HAREBELLS
Campanulaceae *(Campanula* spp.*)*

Identification: Delicate bell-shaped blue to lavender-blue flower (petals partially fused) on delicate stem, with delicate, simple, and extremely narrow leaves. Leaves are alternate. Plant grows 8"–12" tall when mature and blooms April–August, depending on latitude and altitude (and possibly attitude).

Harebells

Habitat: Found in drier foothills and benches of western mountains. Quickly found on the American Serengeti, the broad overreaching meadows of the Lamar River valley in Yellowstone. (Forgot your fly rod? Too bad.)

Food uses: Boil or sauté roots—a fireside nibble. When hiking I eat a flower or two, just to say I did it.

Medicinal uses: Infusion of eastern species used by Native Americans to treat whooping cough and tuberculosis.

LICORICE
Fabaceae *(Glycyrrhiza lepidota)*

Licorice

Identification: Perennial, 3' tall (+/-), with pinnately divided compound leaves and 11–19 leaflets. Leaflets are lance shaped to about 1½" in length. Flowers are yellowish to green-white, pealike to ½", bearing a burrlike fruit that is brown, covered with Velcro-like bristles, indicative of the plant.

Habitat: Found in moist, well-drained areas. A favorite foraging spot is near the riverside campground along the edges of the North Fork of the Shoshone, just above Buffalo Bill Reservoir in Wyoming, 10 miles west of Cody.

Food uses: Like Oriental licorice, the roots are eaten raw or roasted in moderation, and then pounded and sucked or eaten—use to flavor desserts and confections. Glycyrrhizin in the root is sweeter than sugar and said to quench thirst. Like the Oriental variety, use this herb in moderation, as its chemistry is steroidal and may raise blood pressure.

Medicinal uses: Chewed leaves applied as poultice. Root used to settle stomach, a soothing demulcent for the digestive tract. Root also used to treat ulcers and arthritis. Like Oriental variety, used to regulate menses. Raw root juice gargled to reduce toothache. Mucilaginous root soothes throat and suppresses coughs. Steroidal-like compounds in root act similar to store-purchased licorice in Asian markets.

> *CAUTION: Prolonged or substantive use may raise blood pressure and have other undesirable steroidal effects.*

MARSH MARIGOLD; ELKSLIP
Ranunculaceae *(Caltha leptosepala)*

Western marsh marigold

Identification: Fleshy basal leaves, oblong and heart-shaped leaves. Flowers white or white and bluish tinged to 1½" in diameter, 5 oval, oblong petallike sepals (no petals) borne on a 5"–7" tall, sturdy stem. Yellow reproductive parts: pistils, stamens.

Habitat: This plant is abundant in western high places, along the edges of streams and seeps and alpine potholes, ponds, and lakes, often in 1"–2" of water. Find it on the trail along East Hyalite Creek in Hyalite Canyon and in the wet subalpine edges of the Bighorns. Also available in the upper reaches of Cache Creek, Yellowstone, and wet remote areas of the Cascades.

Food uses: Boil leaves and roots in 2 changes of water, then sauté in oil, margarine, or butter. Many sources finish the greens with sour cream or whole cream sauce.

Note: Triple-cooking leaves and roots reduces the toxic glycosides in the plant.

Medicinal uses: Masticated plant (aerial parts) applied to wounds (poultice) to reduce inflammation.

MINER'S LETTUCE
Portulacaceae *(Claytonia perfoliata)*

Miner's lettuce

Identification: Leaves form cup or saucer around stems; delicate, small, white flowers. Found in moist, shady places.

Habitat: Pacific coastal range, east to plains. Particularly abundant near seeps in slot canyons of Utah and along river and stream banks in Montana; tolerates shade.

Food uses: Cook like dandelion greens, or eat leaves and stems raw. Best cut into salads and laced with balsamic vinegar. High in vitamin A. Goes well with curly dock as a steamed green.

Medicinal uses: Tasty survival food, high in nutrients; used as an appetite stimulant.

MINTS OF THE WEST
Lamiaceae *(Mentha arvensis,* other *Mentha* spp.)*

Identification: Aromatic herbs; leaves serrated (toothed); flowers in heads or flowers in stem axils, as in *M. arvensis*; stems square; flowers in clusters.

Habitat: Seeps, streamside, along hiking trails where water runs off, creeks, springs.

Note: The pictured mint was found on the climber's route in the Grand Tetons—a wonderful variety: fragrant and tasty.

Food uses: Add to sauces, pizzas, all bean dishes, chicken soup. Chew as a breath cleanser or brain stimulator. Add to game marinades; try leaves or flowers in bread and pancake batters.

Medicinal uses: Energizing tea, improves circulation to brain, helps ease altitude sickness—although thyme tea is more effective. Tea also cooling, lowers fever.

Mint, Tetons, Wyoming

Mentha arvensis, Alpine, Montana

OXEYE DAISY
Compositae (*Chrysanthemum leucanthemum*)

Identification: Large daisy flower with white petals (up to 3" wide) and yellow center. Basal leaves are spoon shaped with long stems (petioles); teeth on leaf margins are round toothed. Leaves on upper mature plant lack petioles. Plant grows to 2'–3' and blooms throughout the summer. Early spring basal cluster of leaves are choice edibles.

Oxeye daisy

Habitat: Found along roadsides, highways and byways, waste ground, meadows and fields; prefers drier areas. This European import has become widespread and a nuisance in the West. Get on your knees and start eating.

Food uses: Young basal leaves (which grow in abundance) are delicious freshly picked in salads or sautéed—closely approximating the flavor of romaine and Bibb lettuce. Eat in abundance—the locals and ranchers want to get rid of the weed.

Medicinal uses: Eating leaves and drinking leaf tea are diuretic and may act as an antihistamine to help relieve allergies and consequential mucus production. Leaves applied to wounds have a hemostatic quality and stem bleeding.

PINEAPPLE WEED
Compositae *(Matricaria matricarioides)*

Identification: Unlike cultivated chamomile, the domestic herb, pineapple weed has flowers without small white rays (petals) and a large yellow center of reproductive parts. It is spreading, many branched, with severely cut leaves; rayless flowers are conspicuous and pineapple scented, unmistakable.

Habitat: Widespread, along roadsides and in gravel roadways, pathways, waste ground, low- and highly impacted soils, throughout the country east to west, especially in the Northwest and mountainous areas of Montana, Wyoming, Idaho, and Utah.

Food uses: As a tea, fresh flowers preferred over dried. Fresh pineapple weed is more powerful than chamomile. Leaves are edible but bitter. Native Americans pulverized the dried plant and mixed it with meat and berries as a preservative.

Medicinal uses: Pioneers drank the fresh-flower tea as an antispasmodic carminative to aid digestion, prevent ulcers, and relieve arthritis pain. The tea, said to soothe the nerves, may relieve toothache pain. Native Americans used the herb in the same way, primarily for relieving stomach pain, and they considered it a female plant, to be applied wet on hot rocks in a sweat lodge as a soothing aromatic—inviting in the good spirits. Infusion of herb used to relieve menstrual cramps and relieve cold symptoms. Chamomile is widely used topically to treat abrasions, inflammations, eczema, and acne with varied success. One study suggests azulene in chamomile may stimulate liver regeneration. British scientists

Pineapple weed

purport chamomile stimulates infection-fighting macrophages and B-lymphocytes of the human immune system. Commercial preparations in lotions and ointments used as antiseptic treatment of sore gums, wounds, raw or sore nipples, and other inflammations.

Note: A pineapple weed bath (1 cup flowers in a pair of pantyhose) makes an emollient, moisturizing skin wash. Inhaling the steam may relieve upper respiratory infection (sinusitis): Place ¼ cup fresh flowers in an 8-quart pan (containing 1 quart water off the boil plus fresh flowers). Drape a towel over your head, lower head to water, and inhale for sinus congestion. Washing hair with the tea improves quality and sheen.

> **CAUTION: As with many herbs, there is a paradox here. Although antiallergic for some, pineapple weed may be allergenic to others, anaphylactic to a few. If allergic to ragweed, avoid using this plant.**

PIPSISSEWA
Ericaceae *(Chimaphila umbellata)*

Pipsissewa, Washington State

Identification: Small evergreen shrub to 12" tall. Glossy green leaves in whorls, lance shaped, shiny, toothed. Whitish-pink to rose-colored flowers, about ⅜" across, grow in clusters atop a long stem. Fruit is round.

Habitat: Nationwide in forests, foothills, and montane coniferous woods of Colorado, Wyoming, Montana, Alberta, and British Columbia south to California and east to Maine, south to Florida. Not found in the American Southwest, Kentucky, or Tennessee.

Food uses: The plant is used as a flavoring agent for candy and soft drinks; the leaves and roots are boiled and eaten. Capsule are eaten as a digestive.

Medicinal uses: Tea was used as an expectorant; considered a dermatological, urinary, and orthopedic aid. Tea made from aerial parts was used to treat water retention and kidney and bladder problems. An infusion from the plant was used as an eyewash. The astringent herb was used to treat fevers, stomachaches, backaches, coughs, and sore throats and as a wash for wounds, sores, blisters, and rashes. Fresh leaves were crushed and applied externally to reduce inflammation. Native Americans used the tea to regulate menstruation.

SALSIFY
Asteraceae (*Tragopogon pratensis*, other *Tragopogon* spp.)

Identification: Typically, a yellow flower that grows to 40" or less and is somewhat dandelion-like with a larger fluffy seed head (to 4" wide); rays when in bloom are fewer than a dandelion and more widely spaced. Flower is on the end of square, hollow stem. Flower bracts are often longer than yellow or purple rays. Lance-shaped leaves are up to 12" long and clasp or partially wrap the stem. There are several species that have either yellow or purple flowers. Long taproot is edible. Flower is closed on cloudy days; opens in morning and is often closed in afternoon.

Habitat: Widespread from lower elevations to about 7,000' along roads, in campgrounds, open fields, near streams, and on open hillsides. Found

Roadside salsify, Hyalite Canyon

across the northern Mountain West south to Colorado and northern California, west of the plains to the West Coast. Same and similar species are found in the eastern United States.

Food uses: Leaves and roots are edible. Purple-flowered varieties have best-tasting roots. Leaves best early in the season, depending on latitude and altitude. Roots best in spring and fall.

Medicinal uses: Cold infusion used to cleanse and treat animal bites. Latex sap said to be used as a milk substitute and is cathartic. Infusion of leaves and flowers may relieve an upset stomach.

Note: This plant is common in the Hyalite Canyon Recreation Area, along Hyalite Canyon Road in the dispersed camping areas and national forest campsites. Also look in alpine meadows. Use a hand spade (with effort and patience) to extract root from soil.

SEGO LILY
Liliaceae *(Calochortus nuttallii)*

Identification: Deep-set bulb bears 4"–12" stem with grasslike leaves; flowers to 3" in width, white to cream colored typically, with 3 petals as wide as they are broad. Fruit is a narrow capsule, with 3 compartments bearing seeds.

Habitat: Found in dry montane areas from lower elevations to the timberline.

Sego lily, Bighorns, Wyoming

Pictured plant found at 8,000' at Devil's Canyon Ranch in the Bighorns. Dryness of the environment and depth of bulb make this a difficult recovery.

Food uses: Credited for saving the Mormon pioneers in the fall of 1848, this survival food provides an edible bulb and edible leaves. But grasslike leaves provide little sustenance. Bulbs are best—peel and eat raw, or, better, wrap in 2 folds of foil and leave in the coals overnight. Come morning, squeeze soft flesh inside an omelet. Hard-fried boletes are excellent with this breakfast. Seeds are ground into powder and used like cattail pollen, inside baked goods. Bulbs can be dried and used throughout winter. Bulbs can be peeled and candied, cooked in jelly, maple syrup, or hypertonic sugar water. Bulbs also edible throughout year, but best harvested in bloom until you can identify the plant in every season.

Medicinal uses: The raw bulbs may boost immune system activity, providing some protection from acute infections like colds and flu. Other than nutritional, no other medicinal uses are documented.

SHOOTING STAR
Primulaceae (*Dodecatheon* spp.)

Shooting star, Alpine, Montana

Identification: Pink to deep purple flower, yellow at base, nodding on a long stem, 1–5 flowers per stem. Flower is dart shaped (thus, shooting star), petals bending backward, whole plant 4"–10" tall. Leaves are ovate and basal.

Habitat: *D. alpinum* (see photo) found to 11,000'; alpine flower preferring moist area along streams, seeps, weeping meadows dripping or draining into mountain lakes and creeks. Seventeen species found throughout the northern mountain ranges from Montana to Washington, California; 2 species east of the Mississippi.

Food uses: Entire plant is edible. Use only in survival situation if lost and without food. Eat leaves raw, roast roots, and munch on flowers. Eating a single flower will not kill the plant but may not be enough to sustain you.

Medicinal uses: Leaf infusion used to treat cold sores.

SITKA VALERIAN
Valerianaceae (*Valeriana sitchensis*)

Identification: Plant to 24" or more; blooms April–July, a terminal cluster of white to cream-colored odiferous flowers. (Not a particularly pleasant odor to many, but I love it—that stink means I'm back on Mount Rainier.) Petals are feathery. Leaves opposite, staggered up the stem, often with several basal leaves.

Habitat: Montane plant, typically found on north-facing slopes; plentiful in alpine meadows and along trails in the Olympics, Cascades, North Cascades, Mount Rainier, Mount Baker, especially along Heliotrope Trail toward the climber's route.

Note: Take the road to the Sunrise Lodge on the north side of Mount Rainier, and walk to the learning center garden to see this plant and many other medicinal plants of the West and Northwest.

Food uses: Edible roots not worth the effort; tea smells like dirty socks. But root tea is a mild sedative (sleep aid). Seeds may be parched and eaten. Prolonged cooking of roots dilutes offensive odor and saps taste—a survival food.

Valerian, Mount Rainier

Medicinal uses: Root of plant in decoction used as a sedative—stress reducing, tension relieving for insomniacs. *V. sitchensis* roots decocted in water also used to treat pain and colds. Poultice of root used to treat cuts, wounds, bruises, and inflammation. Root decoction also used to treat diarrhea.

WESTERN SKUNK CABBAGE
Araceae *(Lysichiton americanus)*

Identification: Large, green to yellow-green, elephant ear–like leaves that are lustrous and waxy in appearance with a "skunky" odor when torn. Much larger leaves than eastern variety; leaves often 3' in length on Vancouver Island (a small child could use one for a sleeping bag). Yellow flower is an archaic showy sheath surrounding a club-like flower spike.

Habitat: Found as undercover in wet woods, swamps, lowlands, wet coastal areas, along the West Coast Trail of Vancouver Island or the San Juan de Fuca Trail out of Sooke on Vancouver Island in British Columbia.

Western skunk cabbage

Food uses: Native Americans ate western skunk cabbage leaves and roots after washing and steaming or pit-cooking to mush-like consistency. Root can be dried, roasted, and ground into flour. Leaves placed over cooking vegetables as a spice. Young leaves, thoroughly dried, then cooked in soups.

Note: Several western tribes ate roots after boiling 8 times. Drying the leaves or roots of western skunk cabbage eliminates some of the peppery, hot taste of the calcium oxalate crystals (raphides), which are toxic and make these plants, when fresh, unsuitable as food. The waxy leaves used as plates to eat from and to line cooking pits and cedar boxes used in cooking. Leaves are typically used to wrap meat and vegetables for pit-style cooking. Also used to store foods and cover fresh berries. Apparently the oxalate does not taint the food when prepared with raw leaves as a lining or covering. Never eat these plants fresh and uncooked. Roots are numerous and tentacle-like.

CAUTION: Calcium oxalate crystals will burn your digestive tract if eaten raw and fresh.

Medicinal uses: Western skunk cabbage used in the same way as eastern variety. Flowers were steamed and placed against joints to treat arthritis. In sweat lodges, warm leaves used as sitting mats to treat arthritis. Poultice of smashed root used on boils and abscesses. Root burned and smoke inhaled for treating nightmares, disrupted sleep, and flu. Leaves used as poultice for burns. Makah tribe chewed raw root to cause abortion. Charcoal of burned plants used on wounds. Steamed roots used to treat arthritis. A liquid extract of skunk cabbage is still used to treat bronchitis and asthma. Plant considered antispasmodic, expectorant, sedative, and diaphoretic.

CAUTION: Use reserved for skilled practitioners only!

Note: Botanical Beach in Port Renfrew, Vancouver Island, British Columbia, has some of the largest-leaved skunk cabbages I have ever seen. The leaf veins are tough enough to make emergency cordage or sutures.

WESTERN SPRING BEAUTY
Portulacaceae *(Claytonia lanceolata)*

Western spring beauty

Identification: This relative of the eastern variety has broader lance-shaped leaves, flowers with 5 petals, petals white or pink (with pink to red veins) borne on sturdier stems, providing a more robust appearance than its eastern cousin. A basal pair with long petioles and narrow basal leaves die young and leave behind the mature plants with 2 broader, opposite leaves, below a stalk bearing 1–5 flowers; blooms April–July depending on latitude and altitude.

Habitat: Take a hike in mid-July from Hyalite Reservoir to Mirror Lake in Montana (trailhead 19 miles south of Bozeman) and discover this plant along the edges of the glacial lake surrounded by cliffs inhabited by mountain goats. Tolerates shade and full sun and prefers moist meadows and wet seeps from snowmelt runoff.

Found from Montana and Wyoming high country to California, Washington, and up to Alaska.

Food uses: Like the eastern variety, the corms are tasty, with a somewhat bitter aftertaste. Eat corms (roots) raw, steamed, or roasted. Leaves are edible raw or cooked; welcome addition to a mountain meadow salad.

Medicinal uses: Nothing in the record. Relaxes my mind when sitting on a log and chewing a corm. (Where's my cave?)

Edible Plants of the Desert

Here are a few plants found in desert and arid environments that have edible parts. Be certain to see the survival section in the front of this book for more desert plants that can provide you with nutrition and hydration.

AGAVE AND AMERICAN CENTURY PLANT
Agavaceae (Agave spp., including American century plant, A. americana)

Agave, Arizona

Identification: Grayish-green desert plant, with long swordlike succulent leaves, to 10' in height—leaves and shape of plant similar to yucca but larger.

Habitat: Extreme southwestern United States, California, Arizona, Nevada, New Mexico, Mexico, Central and South America. Found in arboretums nationwide.

Food uses: American century plant roots are pit-cooked, crushed in water, and fermented. Young leaves are roasted and eaten (or stored). Fruit heads, young buds, and flower stalks are roasted and eaten (I have also eaten the flowers). Mescal agave "leaves" are cut out from center of plant, then "water" from the plant weeps into the hole. A pulque farmer, using a hollow calabash with a cow horn funnel fused to one end, sucks watery sap into the gourd. The sap is fermented in a bucket for 6–7 days then served. Agave water is harvested this way and used as potable drinking water. Every Hispanic worth their salt (and a squirt of lime) grows an agave. Demand for tequila has greatly inflated agave's value. Disease is also threatening the crop, and urban sprawl in Mexico leaves less land available for cultivation. Agave is brewed into pulque, mescal, and tequila, all of which gave me diarrhea as home brews. The core of the tender inner leaves of the plant may be cooked and eaten.

Medicinal uses: Agave water (juice, sap) considered anti-inflammatory, diuretic. The root extraction is an insecticide. Also, the fresh juice may raise metabolism and increase perspiration. Pulque (agave beer), mescal (agave liquor), and tequila (agave elixir) take the pressure off living.

Note: The sap is used for treating and sealing wounds. Hernán Cortés dropped his ax halfway through his thigh and surely would have died had not the Mesoamerican natives stopped the bleeding and sealed the wound with agave sap, honey, and charcoal. The leaf was cut open and the sticky sap applied to the wound; then the wound was bound with *Tradescantia*.

BUFFALO GOURD
Cucurbitaceae (*Cucurbita foetidissima*)

Buffalo gourd, Texas

Identification: Annual, perennial herb (depending on region); hairs on stems often hardened by calcium deposits. Stems trailing or climbing, tendrils generally 1 per node, stems often branched. Leaves simple, alternate, palmately lobed, and veined, with 3"–7" petioles; flowers at nodes, white to off-white or cream colored, and corolla cup shaped, generally 5-lobed. Fruit 3" in diameter, round gourd or melonlike. Many-seeded.

Habitat: Dry plains, semiarid areas of Southwest: Oklahoma, Texas, New Mexico, Arizona, Nevada, California. Found growing along and up fences, or sprawling along the ground. Very large plants covering up to 100 square feet and more.

Food uses: What I call a survival food because of its bitter principle, it produces oily, protein-rich seeds that are edible after preparation. Seeds are 43 percent oil and 35 percent protein, making them an excellent choice for cultivation. Seeds dried, then roasted before eating. Unlike the pulp of the gourd, the seeds do not contain bitter glycosides (cucurbitacins). Be certain to clean all bitter pulp from seeds before roasting. Cook the seeds in oil or on an oil-sprayed pan over an open fire or in the oven. After 15 minutes of cooking, the protease inhibitors in the seeds are deactivated, making the seeds more digestible. Roasted seed coats may be digestible or you may remove them. Like the pumpkin seed, seed coat can be eaten (insoluble fiber) or removed. Seeds, like mesquite pods and seeds, may be dried and ground into flour. Roots are starch rich and may be smashed and then leached of their starch in water. Fibrous cellulose in roots is bitter; remove cellulose from starchy water to improve taste. Root water is fermented into an alcoholic beverage. This plant has commercial potential in arid biomes where there is a need for protein, starch, and oil. Bitterness is a problem with this survival food—if too bitter, do not eat.

WARNING: A potentially toxic plant related to the edible squashes.

Medicinal uses: Dried hollow gourd used as a rhythm instrument in religious rituals. Ritual use may precede 10,000 years. Dried roots used as an emetic. Decoction of root used as a therapy for venereal disease.

Note: Saponins in root create suds when pounded and mixed with water.

MORMON TEA; JOINT FIR AND EPHEDRA
Ephedraceae *(Ephedra viridis, E. sinica)*

Identification: There are several joint fir species. *E. viridis* looks like it has lost all its leaves. It is a yellow-green plant, many jointed and twiggy, 1'–4' tall, with small leaf scales; double-seeded cones in autumn.

Ephedra, Utah

Habitat: Various species are found on dry, rocky soil or sand in dry and desert areas of the United States: Utah, Arizona, western New Mexico, Colorado, Nevada, California, Oregon.

Food uses: Native Americans roasted the seeds and then infused them into tea. Roasted and ground seeds were mixed with corn or wheat flour to make hot mush.

Medicinal uses: *E. viridis*, Mormon tea, was used in infusion as a tonic, a laxative, to treat anemia, to treat backache, to stem diarrhea, for colds, to treat ulcers, and as therapy for the kidneys and bladder. The decoction or infusion considered a cleansing tonic (blood purifier). Dried and powdered stems used externally to treat wounds and sores. Powder moistened and applied to burns. In women's health, tea used by First People to stimulate delayed menstrual flow (dysmenorrhea). Seeds roasted before brewing into tea.

> **WARNING: E. sinica,** *as a cardiovascular stimulant and central nervous system stimulant, may be dangerous for people with elevated blood pressure, heart disease, and/or tachycardia. It is federally regulated and not to be used during pregnancy or by nursing mothers. The import and use of this drug is restricted in several countries. Deaths have been associated with the abuse of this drug (100 mg may be lethal).*

PRICKLY PEAR
Cactaceae *(Opuntia spp.)*

Identification. All species are low growing perennials and have an oval pad with thorny leaves of various sizes. Flowers are yellowish. Fruits are dull red to purple.

Prickly pear, Black Hills, South Dakota

Habitat: Various species found from coast to coast in dry, sometimes sandy areas, even along the East Coast and on dry islands of the Pacific Northwest. The Badlands of South Dakota have prickly pear, as does the Sonoran Desert and dry western regions from British Columbia to central Mexico. Great foraging found along the back roads of Texas.

Food uses: Flowers and flower buds are roasted and eaten. The pads, which are often mistaken for leaves (spines are the leaves), are edible. Plump pads thrown on hot coals and roasted. Fire burns off the spines and cooks the interior. Let cool, then peel the skin and eat the inner core. Stir-fry or chop the pad "meat" into huevos rancheros with yucca blossoms and salsa verde. The fruit when red and ripe is tasty, often made into jelly. Eat

Prickly pear margarita

it out of hand right off plant (remove prickly hairs). The pads mixed with water, sugar, yeast, and fermented into an alcoholic drink. Numerous other cacti are edible (see "Survival Foods" chapter).

Medicinal uses: Flowers are astringent and uses as a poultice over wounds. Flower tea for treating stomach complaints including diarrhea and irritable bowel syndrome. The stem ash applied to burns and cuts. Pima Indians use edible pads for gastrointestinal complaints. Pima stripped spines, cooked, sliced, and placed a poultice of the plant on breasts as a lactagogue. Pads sliced in half and applied as poultice for cleansing and sealing wounds, infections, bites, stings, snake envenomation. Pads scorched of spines, then slit, and moist side placed against the insult/wound. Inner flesh, a chemotactic attractant (surfactant), draws serum from the wound site, cleaning and sealing it. Southwestern practitioners treat scorpion stings and recluse spider bites with slit pads.

SAGE
Asteraceae *(Artemisia tridentata)*

Identification: Gray, fragrant shrub to 7'. Leaves are wedge shaped, lobed (3 teeth), broad at tip, tapering to the base. Yellow and brownish flowers form spreading, long, narrow clusters, blooming July–October. Seed is hairy achene.

Antelope ranging in sage and brushbar

Habitat: Desert plant, found in dry areas of Wyoming, Washington, Montana, Texas, New Mexico, California, Idaho, Oregon, Colorado.

Food uses: Seeds, raw or dried, ground into flour and eaten as a survival food. Seeds added to liqueurs for fragrance and flavor. Use as a spice or flavoring in small amounts as a substitute for salvia sage; good with venison, turkey, and chicken. Often sage is the only source of firewood in the desert. Most varieties of sage seeds used as food by Native Americans.

Medicinal uses: Native American medicine warrior plant used for smudging and sweeping to rid the victim of bad airs and evil spirits. Leaves used as a tea to treat infections and stomachaches and to ease childbirth, or as a wash for sore eyes. Leaves soaked in water and used as a poultice over wounds. Limbs used as switches in sweat baths. Infusion used to treat sore throats, coughs, colds, bronchitis. Decoction or infusion used as a wash for sores, cuts, and pimples. Aromatic decoction of steaming herb inhaled for respiratory ailments and headaches. Decoction said to be internally antidiarrheal and externally antirheumatic. This panacea drug also drunk to relieve constipation. See details on my Native American Medicine DVD free viewing at Jim Meuninck YouTube.

Note: Add this herb to your hot bath, hot tub, or sweat lodge for a fragrant, disinfecting, and relaxing cleanse.

YUCCA
Agavaceae *(Yucca filamentosa,* other *Yucca* spp.)

Yucca

Identification: Common lawn ornamental, with long swordlike leaves to 2'; tough, fibrous, white flowers on a tall flower stalk, central to the plant, a strikingly distinctive attribute.

Habitat: Almost universal in distribution (helped by landscapers and gardeners), various species in mountains, deserts, temperate areas; loves sun, tolerates drought, but does well on drained soil. Found coast-to-coast, north and south.

Food uses: Yucca flowers are edible. The young seedpods may be stir-fried. The flowers picked and sautéed in olive oil. Roll them into an omelet. Attractive addition to a salad, or eat out of hand.

Medicinal uses: Used for liver and gallbladder cleansing.

Note: I use the water extraction of the root to make an organic, water-soluble insect-repelling spray for fruit and vegetables. I spray pears with yucca root water in the spring. The results are excellent. Take about 1 cubic inch of root and blend it in 2 cups water. Strain, filter into sprayer. Add another pint of water and spray directly on buds, flowers, and young pears, apples.

Marine Vegetables

Almost all marine seaweeds are safe to consume, and the 2 questionable varieties are easy to avoid: foul-tasting *Lyngbya*, a thin, hairlike species that clings to mangrove roots in warm subtropical and tropical waters; and *Desmarestia*, which is found in deep, open waters and contains sulfuric acid that imparts an unpleasant lemonlike taste. Therefore, avoid mangrove-clinging seaweeds and deep-open-water varieties.

> **CAUTION: Research suggests some seaweed supplements may contain heavy metals. The fresh or dried whole plant is best.**

Because of limited space, only a few popular edible seaweeds are covered here.

ALARIA
Alariaceae *(Alaria marginata)*

Alaria, Washington coast

Identification: Midrib of large fronds is flattened. Grows to 10' but often smaller, to 12" wide, green to olive-brown, with smaller bladelike leaves at base. Attached to hard surface, rock, old lava flows, etc.

Habitat: Found in lower tidal zones from northern California to Alaska.

Food uses: Midrib is a crunchy treat in the spring (fresh). Blades can be dried or eaten fresh.

Medicinal uses: A multimineral "pill" containing magnesium, phosphorus, boron. High in vitamins C and B12 when eaten fresh. For more see Evelyn McConnaughey's book, *Sea Vegetables*.

BEACH PEA
Fabaceae *(Lathyrus japonicus* var. *maritimus)*

Beach pea, Sooke, British Columbia

Identification: Marine coastal dweller that dawdles along upper littoral area of the beach. Beach pea leaves are compound, even numbered, typically 6–12 leaflets; leaflets tipped with a curling tendril typical of pea family; opposite leaflets about 2½" long. Fruit is pea pod–like and hairy, about 2½" long.

WARNING: Many members of the pea family are potentially toxic. Make positive identification, eat only small amounts of edible wild foods, and follow all foraging rules.

Habitat: Coastal areas of East and West Coasts. Found in sandy upper areas of beach among driftwood and dunes.

Food uses: Cook peas with salmon. Stir-fry, boil, or steam new growth (stalks of spring). After peas flower, tender young pods may be cooked and eaten like snow peas. The Inuit dried peas and roasted them like coffee beans, then percolated.

Medicinal uses: Chinese use peas as tonic for the urinary organs and intestinal tract. Inuit consider the peas poisonous. Coastal Iroquois treated rheumatism with cooked whole young plant.

BLADDERWRACK; FUCUS; SEA WRACK
Fucaceae *(Fucus gardneri, F. vesiculosus)*

Bladderwrack, Vancouver Island, British Columbia

Identification: Bladderwrack, or fucus, is a perennial seaweed that thrives in wave-sheltered to moderately exposed conditions. The plant reaches 16" in length and consists of many branches with little inflated bulbs at their tips. The gas-filled vesicles on each side of the midrib vein float the plant in an upright position from its holdfast anchorage, enabling the plant to absorb nutrition and sunlight. Although a brown algae, color ranges from green to brown.

Habitat: A cold-water seaweed found in both the sublittoral (exposed at low tide) and the deeper littoral tidal zones. It ranges in the Atlantic Ocean from New Jersey to Maine and north; in the Pacific Ocean from California to Alaska. Gather from clean water free of heavy metals and other pollution. Forage at low tide in wave-sheltered coves and rocky niches.

Food uses: A common food in Japan; used as an additive and flavoring in various food products in Europe. It is dried and made into a nutritious tea and added to soups, particularly Japanese- and Chinese-style noodle soups. It flavors stews, fortifying them with iodine. I like to put a dried piece in my mouth and suck on it until soft, and then chew and swallow. For landlocked Midwesterners, the seaweed is available at Asian markets.

Medicinal uses: Bladderwrack is a component of tablets or powders used as nutritional supplements. It contains concentrations of iodine and is used as a treatment for hypothyroidism (underactive thyroid gland) and obesity. (***Note:*** Amounts of iodine in supplements vary, making this a dubious use.) Bladderwrack contains alginic acid that swells upon contact with water. When taken orally, it forms a seal at the top of the stomach and is sold over the counter as a heartburn treatment and bulking laxative. Natural health enthusiasts also use the plant to treat dysmenorrhea.

KELP
Laminariaceae *(Laminaria* spp.*)*

Kelp, Straits of San Juan

Identification: A brown seaweed that can grow to more than 100' in length. Large frond-like leaves; stem can be thick as a human's wrist; air-filled bulbs or bladders hold plant erect in water. Plant torn loose and washed ashore after storms.

Habitat: Found along the West Coast, from California to Alaska, in 10'–100' of water.

Food uses: Excellent food for fiber and contains most minerals humans need. Wash the plant in clean water. Soak in weak wine vinegar or lemon juice until pliable. Air-dry in sun. After drying, scrape off blue-green surface layer. Kelp's thick white core can be chopped, shredded, or ground—best cooked in soups and stews. Dry the shredded parts for later use. I have dried various seaweeds by spreading them on my car windshield in full sunlight.

Medicinal uses: Improves yolk color and calcium content when fed to chickens. Good source of iodine (important clotting agent). Kelp salt prevents muscle cramps.

Note: Gardeners are encouraged to spread seaweeds of all types on their organic gardens. Containing more than 90 minerals, marine algae are a wonderful addition to the garden.

NORI; LAVER
Bangiaceae *(Porphyra* spp.*)*

Nori, Pacific coast

Identification: Numerous species in various tints and colors from red to purple, gray, and black (with age). Shape is irregular and fans (spans) to 20"; species vary from roundish to oval, to oblong and spade-like. Thin and elastic, membranous thin blades lie flat, seeking the form of the rock, and have a ruffled appearance, satin sheen.

Habitat: Intertidal zone from Oregon to Alaska; found in rocky or sandy areas.

Food uses: Tasty, nutritious, and available in Asian markets. Chew fresh or cook with soy and lime juice. Dried it may be used as a vitamin-rich crumble in salads and over other dishes requiring salt. Sauté fresh and then add to pizza. Dry and flake into baked goods; use in soups and stews.

Medicinal uses: High in vitamins, especially vitamin A. May lower hypertension; fat lowering by inhibiting production of lipase and may reduce the absorption of fat.

NARROW-LEAFED SEASIDE PLANTAIN; GOOSE TONGUE
Plantaginaceae *(Plantago maritima)*

Identification: Long, narrow, lance-shaped leaves growing from basal whorl; no basal sheath; leaves with thick longitudinal ribs. Plant's appearance is similar to narrow-leafed garden plantain (*P. lanceolata*).

> **WARNING: Goose tongue can be confused with arrow grass: Arrow grass leaves are flat on one side and round on the other, with sheaves at the base of the leaves. Goose tongue leaves have prominent ribs and are more flattened. If you cut the goose tongue leaf in cross section, it would appear flat or slightly V-shaped. The characteristic plantain spike of goose tongue is distinctive. Remember Wild Plant Foraging Rule #1: Follow these 2 plants through an entire season before eating goose tongue.**

Habitat: West Coast of North America. Upper tidal zone or shoreline, often submerged at high tide.

Food uses: Succulently salty and mineral rich. Eat it fresh and raw. Also used as a stuffing for salmon: Mix it with finely sliced kelp, and sauté it with olive oil and water. Then stuff the mixture in the cavity of a cleaned and washed salmon and steam the fish in a reed basket or in a Chinese basket steamer over a pot of boiling water until done.

Goose tongue

Medicinal uses: Fresh leaves and fresh juice considered anti-inflammatory and antimicrobial. Native American healer Patsy Clark chews the leaves and then applies them over wounds. In Germany leaves are simmered in honey for 20 minutes to treat gastric ulcers.

SEA ASPARAGUS; AMERICAN GLASSWORT

Chenopodiaceae *(Salicornia virginica, S. maritima)*

Identification: Fleshy mats. Individual plants grow from slender rhizomes; leaves are absent, reduced to tiny opposite scales; leafless stems are prostrate or erect, many jointed, with numerous flowering stems growing upright from the main stem; plant stems generally brown-purple. Eastern variety is emerald green in spring to red in late summer.

Sea asparagus

Habitat: Coastal areas, beaches, salt marshes in the upper tidal zone from Washington State north in the West and Nova Scotia south in the East.

Food uses: Wash and eat stems raw or cooked—salty. Eat like asparagus. Boil, sauté, or fry young stems. Older stems are not tender. Fresh plant can be purchased in seafood and grocery stores on the Washington and British Columbia coasts. Native Americans dried and ground the plant and used it like flour in cakes and bread, typically sweetened with honey. Stems eaten as food by Salish, Heiltsuk, and Goshute First People.

Medicinal uses: External use (whole aerial parts of plants) by Heiltsuk people to treat edema, pain, arthritis, and rheumatism.

Caution: All edible ocean plants found in contaminated coastal waters may contain toxins and should be eaten in moderation. Kelp and other sea vegetables contain iodine; eat in moderation.

Appendix A: Poisonous Plants

Here a few poisonous plants are identified. Several of these plants have long traditions in natural medicine but are best reserved for the skilled hands of a knowledgeable holistic health-care practitioner. See the FalconGuide *Medicinal Plants of North America* and *Poisonous and Psychoactive Plants* (both by this author) for detailed information. As mentioned earlier, many members of the buttercup family are considered toxic, and although a few varieties are eaten, I recommend that you avoid them, as they are a novelty food and not particularly good tasting.

AMERICAN LIVERWORT
Ranunculaceae *(Hepatica americana)*

Liver-shaped leaves with hairy petioles; one of the first flowers of spring. Toxic alkaloid—avoid eating the plant.

ARROW ARUM
Araceae *(Peltandra virginica)*

Arrow-shaped leaf, pinnate veins; green, primitive-looking flower; grows in water. All parts of the plant, including the flower and mature fruit, are toxic. Compare the leaf veins of arrow arum with those of edible duck potato (arrowhead).

BANEBERRY, RED AND WHITE; BUGBANE
Ranunculaceae *(Actaea rubra, A. pachypoda)*

A. pachypoda has more rounded white flower clusters than *A. rubra*. Baneberry contains toxins that have an immediate sedative effect on human cardiac muscle. Ingestion of the berries can lead to cardiac arrest.

BITTERSWEET NIGHTSHADE
Solanaceae *(Solanum dulcamara)*

Climbing vine, found clinging to shrubs in wetlands; purple rocket-shaped flowers, bearing a reddish-orange fruit with leaves lobed and alternate. Consumption rarely fatal.

BLUEFLAG; WILD IRIS
Iridaceae *(Iris versicolor)*

Wetland plant with swordlike leaves; rhizome grows to about 3'. Stems typically have a gray-blue tint and are flat. Flower is orchidlike (irregular), blue to violet. Found in damp marshes, fens, bogs, along streams and the edges of lakes.

BUCKEYE; HORSE CHESTNUT
Hippocastanaceae *(Aesculus hippocastanum)*

Medium-size tree, 50' to 80' tall. Leaves compound with 5 leaflets, fine toothed. Fruit has husk with thick knobby spines covering a shiny brown seed. Dried leaves and nut oil used as medicine. Nut is not edible. Active compounds are triterpene saponins, rutin, quercitrin, isoquercitrin.

BUCKTHORN; CASCARA SAGRADA
Rhamnaceae *(Rhamnus* spp., *R. purshiana)*

Small shrubs or trees, 4'–20' tall, many branched and densely foliated. When mature, bark is gray-brown with gray-white lenticels (spots). Leaves are thin, bladelike, and hairy on the ribs, fully margined, elliptical to ovate, and 2" in length. Greenish-white flowers are

numerous and grow on axillary cymes. Flowers are very small, 5 petals. Ripe fruit is red to black-purple with 2 or 3 seeds. *R. purshiana* is taller, to 30', with leaves that have 20–24 veins. White flowers are in clusters. *R. purshiana* grows in the foothills of British Columbia, Idaho, Washington, Montana, and Oregon.

CLEMATIS; WESTERN BLUE VIRGINSBOWER
Ranunculaceae (*Clematis occidentalis*)

A climbing vine of Montana and other mountain regions, as well as 26 other states. Toothed leaves in sets of 3, blue nodding flower with 4 petals, roughly bell-shaped blossom when closed. Contains anemonin, a toxic alkaloid that causes severe pain in the mouth if eaten and skin irritation if touched. If inhaled, symptoms include burning sensation of mouth and mouth ulcers.

DATURA; JIMSONWEED
Solanaceae (*Datura stramonium, D. meteloides*)

Trumpetlike flower is distinctive. Seed capsule studded with spines. Flowers white to light violet. Leaves are toothed, coarse textured. Found along roadsides and in bean and corn fields throughout the United States. *D. meteloides*, with white to pinkish flowers, is more common in the Southwest and Four Corners and is a popular, showy garden flower throughout the Midwest.

DUTCHMAN'S BREECHES
Papaveraceae (*Dicentra cucullaria*)

Deeply dissected leaves without a stalk; white flower looks like a man's breeches. Tuber is toxic. Rarely fatal, may cause convulsions.

FOXGLOVE; PURPLE FOXGLOVE
Scrophulariaceae *(Digitalis purpurea)*

Biennial 3'–5' with lance-shaped, fuzzy leaves in basal rosette that looks somewhat like mullein leaves or comfrey leaves—rarely dock leaves—but the leaves of digitalis are toxic. Thimble-shaped white to purple flowers on a spike. They look like gloves, hence the name. Flowers bloom in summer of second year. Common mountain wildflower, found along roadsides in the Northwest and eastern mountain states.

HELLEBORE, FALSE
Liliaceae *(Veratrum viride)*

Large, ovate, stalkless leaves, clinging and spiraling up sturdy stem; yellow-green flowers in branched clusters. In East grows in wet, swampy areas; in West found on open mountain slopes. Potentially fatal if eaten.

HEMLOCK, POISON
Umbelliferae *(Conium maculatum)*

Purple-spotted, hollow stems; grows to 6'–7' with white flowers in umbels that are either flat or umbrella shaped. Leaves are divided parsley-like into small leaflets (leaves, too). Plant has many characteristics of edible members of the parsley family. Ingestion of the toxin coniine can be and often is fatal.

HORSE NETTLE
Solanum *(Solanum carolinense)*

Leaves and stems with spines. Leaves
coarse, irregular, large toothed. White
flower with yellow reproductive parts.
The alkaloid solanum causes vomiting,
stomach and bowel pain.

JACK-IN-THE-PULPIT; INDIAN TURNIP
Araceae *(Arisaema triphyllum)*

Flower is a spathe and spadix, and with
little imagination you see a preacher in
a pulpit. A dangerous and contraceptive herb if not prepared properly—and
even at that, not palatable.

LARKSPUR, WESTERN
Ranunculaceae *(Delphinium glaucum)*

A poisonous plant defined by the
flower color, evident spur, and shape
of leaves (deeply cut). Various species
found throughout the United States.
D. glaucum found in moist areas in the
Mountain West.

LOBELIA; INDIAN TOBACCO; PUKEWEED

Campanulaceae *(Lobelia siphilitica, other Lobelia spp.)*

Once used to treat syphilis, this member of the bluebell family has showy blue flowers about 1" in size found in leaf axils. Various species found across the continent in woods, meadows, wetlands, mountains. Tubular and lipped flower is indicative. Toxic alkaloids.

MAYAPPLE

Berberidaceae *(Podophyllum peltatum)*

Woodland plant creates ground cover of large umbrellalike leaves. Parasollike leaf deeply dissected, with a single white flower bearing an edible fruit in July. All other parts of the plant are toxic. Ingestion may lead to coma and death.

MILKWEED

Asclepiadaceae *(Asclepias syriaca, other Asclepias spp.)*

Stomach-shaped seedpod, large ovate leaves that exude milklike sap when damaged. Although flowers, young shoots, and seedpods are edible with proper cooking (2 changes of water, then sauté), the toxic substance is a cardiac glycoside, and there are numerous other, safe plant choices.

MOONSEED
Menispermaceae *(Menispermum canadense)*

Climbing vine with green stems, toxic berries red when ripe, leaves round or heart shaped with a pointed tip; if not round, showing 3 shallow lobes (6"–10" wide). Unripe green fruit may be confused with wild grapes; ripe fruit is red—moon-shaped crescent on seed indicative—pluck seed from fruit to discover the crescent.

POISON IVY
Anacardiaceae *(Toxicodendron radicans)*

Shrub or climbing hairy vine, leaflets in 3s, with white or pale yellow berries; contact causes dermatitis. Rub with jewelweed to reduce redness and itching. A thorough scrubbing with soap and water within an hour of contact prevents this discomfort.

POISON SUMAC
Anacardiaceae *(Rhus vernix)*

Shrub with compound leaves, 7–15 leaflets with white fruit (berries dangling from delicate stems). Causes contact dermatitis.

POKEWEED
Phytolaccaceae *(Phytolacca americana)*

Ovate leaves, pointed at tip; purple stem when mature; elongated clusters of purple berries. The plant grows in gardens, wastelands, vacant lots, and along the fringes of woods. Young green leaves are edible after cooking in change of water and then sautéing; pick before stems turn purple for maximum safety. Causes cramps and vomiting.

SKUNK CABBAGE, EASTERN AND WESTERN
Araceae *(Lysichiton americanus)*

Large, green, elephant ear–like leaves that are lustrous and waxy in appearance with a "skunky" odor when torn. Found as undercover in wet woods, swamps, lowlands east and west of the Rockies. Flower is an archaic showy sheath surrounding club-like flower spike. Avoid using the fresh parts of

this plant as food or medicine. Western variety has yellow flower; large, up to 3' leaves, waxy sheen; grows in colonies. Contains caustic oxalate crystals (raphides), which are toxic and make these plants unsuitable as food.

WATER HEMLOCK
Umbelliferae *(Cicuta maculata)*

Found near wetlands. Has sharply toothed leaves, white umbrella-shaped flower clusters, hollow stems. In many ways similar to poison hemlock in appearance—and like a few of its edible family members. Distinctive is the leaf venation, which terminates within the marginal notches.

Note: Veins on water hemlock terminate at the notch instead of the tip. This is indicative.

YAUPON; YAUPON HOLLY
Aquifoliaceae *(Ilex vomitoria)*

Yaupon is an evergreen holly, shrub-like with glossy green leaves that have sharp points. Found in Texas and throughout the Southwest. Berries are toxic, not edible.

Appendix B: Recipes

The secret to successful wild-plant cooking is to start with traditional recipes that you enjoy. Try a dandelion leaf on a hamburger. Stuff miner's lettuce in an omelet. Add burdock root and Jerusalem artichokes to stew. Add a sprig or two of wild mint to chicken and bean soups. Substitute what is available for what is in the following recipes. Become a wild-foods wizard. You'll be rewarded with a long, happy, and healthy life.

Guascas Soup

This is a delicious traditional potato, corn, and chicken soup from South America.

SERVES 6

Guascas Soup

- Unsalted butter and/or olive oil, for sautéing
- All-purpose flour, for dusting chicken
- 6 chicken thighs (or 8 legs)
- 1 large onion, diced
- ½ cup finely chopped and lightly packed gallant soldier flower heads and leaves
- 64 ounces chicken broth
- 2 pounds potatoes, cubed
- 4 ears sweet corn
- 3 tablespoons soy sauce (optional)
- 3 tablespoons dry white wine (optional)
- 2 avocados, diced
- ½ cup fresh coriander leaves
- 36 capers
- Sprig of wild mint per bowl
- Sour cream
- Salt and pepper to taste

Preparation: Sauté chopped flour-dusted chicken, onion, and gallant soldiers. Save a few flowers for garnish. Add chicken broth to 5-quart soup pot. Transfer the onion, chicken, and soldiers to the broth. Brown the potatoes and add to pot. Simmer until the chicken is done; remove the chicken, cool, and then shred. Add corn to soup and simmer to thicken. At this point, I like to add 3 tablespoons each of soy and white wine. After the soup has been reduced, long enough to soften the corn (7 or 8 minutes), ladle into dishes. Add the shredded chicken and garnish with avocado, fresh coriander leaves, capers, and a sprig of mint atop a dollop of sour cream. Sprinkle a few gallant soldier flowers on top, season to taste with salt and pepper, and serve.

Fiddlehead Tacos

Serves 4

Fiddleheads can be simmered in chicken stock (or water) for 7 to 8 minutes and then transferred to a pan and sautéed. Let cool and add to salads or soups. Or try a fiddlehead taco.

4 or 5 fiddleheads
½ cup chicken broth, plus extra for simmering
1 package taco seasoning mix
Diced onions
Diced tomatoes
3 roasted chicken thighs, chopped
Flour tortillas
Mayonnaise
Red salsa
1 cup grated cheese (I prefer Asiago, although it dominates.)

Fiddlehead Tacos

Preparation: Simmer the fiddleheads in chicken broth for 7 to 8 minutes; let them cool, then chop and dice. In a sauté pan, combine the taco seasoning and ½ cup of the chicken broth. Add the diced fiddleheads, onions, tomatoes, and chopped chicken thighs. Cook until liquid disappears. Spread onto a flour tortilla lathered with mayonnaise and red salsa; sprinkle on cheese. Get a grip and enjoy.

Hairy Cress Scramble

Serves 4

½ cup chopped hairy bittercress leaves and petals
7 or 8 eggs, beaten
Dash of milk
2 tablespoons unsalted butter
8 mushrooms (I prefer black trumpets or chopped oysters.)
2 peeled and boiled potatoes, mashed
Salt, pepper, or Lawry's salt to taste

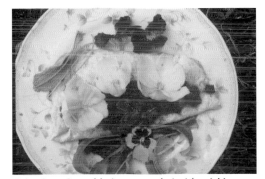

Hairy Cress Scramble (as an omelet) with prickly pear blossoms

Preparation: In a bowl combine the chopped cress, eggs, and milk. Set aside. Over medium heat, melt the butter; add the mushrooms and sauté for 2 minutes. Add the potatoes and sauté for 2 more minutes, then pour in the beaten egg and chopped cress mixture. Scramble to preferred doneness. (**Note:** This could be made into an omelet instead of a scramble.) Season to taste and serve. **Option:** Substitute stinging nettle and chickweed for hairy bittercress.

Jungle Berry Toast
The best way to preserve and enjoy a fruit year-round is to make it into a jam or jelly.

Toast wedges: blackberry, elderberry, pawpaw, and autumn olive, drizzled with maple syrup

Autumn olive makes a terrific jelly. Blackberry is second to none. Scoop pawpaw fruit from its skin and spread it on toast. Gather elderberries, cook a pound and a half of elderberries down to a pint of juice, and strain away the skin and seeds; add pectin, sugar, lemon juice, teaspoon of butter. These recipes and 100 more are available at Jim Meuninck's YouTube channel. Also search Jim Meuninck Trees, Shrubs, Nuts and Berries.

Paleo Greens
SERVES 4

Paleo Greens sandwich

Combine 1 cup each of chopped lovage and, if desired, French sorrel leaves. Remember, dock, nettle, and watercress are available throughout the year. Miner's lettuce, nuts, and fruit are welcome additions to this dish. Experiment!

Combine chopped greens in a pan with ½ cup water, 3 tablespoons butter or olive oil, and 1 teaspoon reduced-sodium soy sauce; cover, steam for 2 to 3 minutes; toss twice. For added flavor, add chopped cooked bacon or chopped smoked ham.

Crepe de Lasceau
SERVES 2

½ cup cattail pollen
2 cups prepared pancake batter
Morels, chopped
Unsalted butter
Violet petals
Maple syrup
Sour cream
Black walnuts, raspberries, blueberries, and/or mulberries
Optional: Bacon, sausage, ham

Crepe de Lasceau variation with blueberry, spearmint blossoms, hickory nuts, and autumn olive butter

Preparation: Stir cattail pollen into thin pancake batter; set aside. Sauté morels in butter in a small pan. Cook a thin pancake (or crepe) in a pan; add chopped morels and violet petals. Roll crepe, wet with syrup, and plop—on goes the sour cream.

Sprinkle with black walnuts and berries. Serve with bacon, sausage, or ham, if desired.

Piltdown Pizza
SERVES 4

Ingredients: Pizza dough and sauce (recipes below), cattail pollen, wild greens (nettle, leeks, dandelion, plantain, garden sorrel, dock, burdock), oyster or other available mushrooms, oats, and flaxseed. Use about ½ cup each of greens and 1½ cups sautéed mushrooms (whole or chopped). If you are foraging out West, add bistort, chiming bells, fireweed shoots, and geraniums.

Delicious, even in a dark, damp cave

Pizza dough: Mix 3 cups each of white and whole wheat flours; add ¼ cup flaxseeds, 1 tablespoon rolled oats, and 1 cup cattail male reproductive parts. Add 2 tablespoons instant yeast to about 2 cups warm water. While mixing dough, add yeast water and 1 tablespoon olive oil. Mix until you have a nice semidry, spongy ball. Divide ball into 3 pieces to make 3 pizzas; freeze what you don't use.

Sauce: For 1 pizza, use one (16-ounce) can diced tomatoes. Pour into a saucepan and add basil, garlic, oregano, dill (to taste, about ½ teaspoon of each), and 1 teaspoon pickle juice. Simmer to thicken.

Roll out dough in pizza pan and bake at 500°F for about 3 minutes. Pull from oven and add sauce and chopped wild foods, including wild leeks (wild foods may be raw or cooked). Sprinkle on a combination of your favorite pizza cheeses. Return to 500°F oven and cook for 12 minutes, or until cheese melts and browns. Serve at once.

Neanderthal Buzz
This dish works well with oxeye daisy leaves and spring beauty corms.
SERVES 2

Ingredients: 3 cups watercress, 2 cups woodland or garden sorrel (or substitute French sorrel), 1 cup chopped celery or young lovage leaves, 6 chopped leeks (more if you date or are married to a Cro-Magnon), 1 tablespoon soy sauce, 3 tablespoons butter, 3 tablespoons

Neanderthal Buzz

olive oil, 4 cups chicken broth (or mammoth broth if available), cup sour cream, salt and pepper to taste.

Preparation: Sauté all greens and vegetables in soy sauce, butter, and olive oil. Add greens and vegetables to broth, simmer for 5 minutes; cool, stir in sour cream—eat cold in a cave, or reheat over the campfire and slurp. Adding powdered mushrooms will change the taste of this soup but not the pleasure of eating it.

Hint: Top soup with several wild mulberries.

Frittata Archaeopteryx

Serves 4–6

  1 cup chopped nettle leaves
  ¾ cup chopped leeks with leaves
  ½ cup curly dock leaves
  ½ cup raw purslane
  ½ cup chopped watercress
  Olive oil, for sautéing
  10 slices Jerusalem artichokes
  7 thin (or sliced) spears wild asparagus
  1 cup morels and/or sautéed wood ear mushrooms
  ½ cup mozzarella
  ½ cup grated Parmesan cheese, plus more for the top
  6 eggs, beaten
  Salsa, for serving

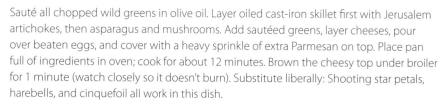

Frittata with Jerusalem artichokes

Preparation: Preheat oven to 375°F.

Sauté all chopped wild greens in olive oil. Layer oiled cast-iron skillet first with Jerusalem artichokes, then asparagus and mushrooms. Add sautéed greens, layer cheeses, pour over beaten eggs, and cover with a heavy sprinkle of extra Parmesan on top. Place pan full of ingredients in oven; cook for about 12 minutes. Brown the cheesy top under broiler for 1 minute (watch closely so it doesn't burn). Substitute liberally: Shooting star petals, harebells, and cinquefoil all work in this dish.

Serve with fresh or prepared salsa. (For more details see Tortilla Española recipe, page 150.)

Velociraptor Pie

Serves 4–6

  1 cup each: 2 strong-flavored grated cheeses
    (Asiago, Jarlsberg, Romano, Parmesan,
    etc.) for 2 cups total grated (I know,
    I know; it's a lot of cheese, but we
    prehominids don't even know what a
    heart attack is, and we work all the time.)
  Generous additions of oregano, fennel leaves,
    basil
  1 cup each: sautéed nettle leaves, dock
    leaves, watercress, leek leaves; seasonal
    mushrooms—oyster and puffballs work great in combination (This is a mix-and-match creation—put in what is available, and see what happens.)
  4 sheets phyllo dough
  Cooking spray or butter

Phyllo dough and wild greens

Preparation: Mix grated cheeses and seasonings with sautéed wild vegetables and spoon all into the phyllo dough nest. Fold over tips of phyllo dough to cover the vegetables, and then spray or brush the top with butter. Preheat oven and cook at 375°F for 10–12 minutes until dough is light brown.

Stuffed Olives

Only a miserly Mousterian could come up with this: Buy a jar of "party stuffer olives." Pour pickling juice from the jar into a saucepan, bring to a boil. Meanwhile, stuff olives with sliced bits of Jerusalem artichokes. Drop the stuffed olives back into the jar, pour boiling hot pickle juice over—the jar will self-seal—and keep refrigerated. Have dill pickling juice left over from a pickle jar? Then reheat to a boil

Stuffed olives

and drop in all of the above. Pickled wild foods enhance eggs, pizzas, sauces, soup (*sopa*) and salsas—in any language the flavor is terrific.

Options: Burdock root, spring beauty corms, fireweed flowers, pokeweed greens, cattail shoots, mushrooms can all be stuffed and pickled.

Lucy's Lasagna
Here is a modern twist on humankind's oldest recipe, created by our first mother: Lucy of the Rift Valley.
Serves 4–6

Take your favorite lasagna recipe, but instead of spinach, add sautéed leeks, dock, watercress, and strips of burdock root—also oregano, basil, dill and fennel seeds, salt, and pepper for

Lasagna with wild leeks and dock leaves

seasoning. Stronger cheeses are best, and load up on sautéed mushrooms in season. Nuts and wild rice help this formula too.

Bake for 45 minutes in a preheated 375°F oven.

Useful tip: First mix cheeses (e.g., ricotta, Parmesan, and cottage) together with spices and seasoning. Layer the cheese blend with a mixture of canned (or fresh) crushed plum tomatoes and a can of tomato sauce (fresh, organic, and local is best—ask any Neanderthal).

Homo Habilis Hontzontles

SERVES 1–2

3 fresh chicken eggs
4 lamb's-quarter flower spikes (stems)
    with seeds and leaves per person
    (or, a few weeks earlier in the
    season, cut flower spikes, about 10
    inches long)
All-purpose flour, for dusting
Canola or peanut oil, for frying
Salsa—green and red and local
    (imported is fine)
1 can (16 ounces) black beans

Need lamb's-quarter, salsa, beans, mint flowers, Asiatic dayflowers, and evening primrose blossoms

½ half cup each: blackberries, sunflower petals, and/or jewelweed blossoms
Salt and pepper

Preparation: Beat eggs; dredge lamb's-quarter seed heads through eggs until thoroughly soaked. Sift a thin sheen of flour over egg batter; fry in ½ inch of oil until brown. Drain on paper towels. Arrange on plate with salsa and black bean sides; garnish with blackberries and sunflower petals and/or jewelweed blossoms.

Optional: A side dish of wild rice and chopped leeks, stirred into salsa, supports enthusiasm for this recipe.

Mushroom Sauce Australopithecine

Crush air-dried puffballs into a powder. When reconstituted with water or broth, this white powder makes a strong-flavored sauce—unbeatable.

SERVES 4–6

Any gravy mix will work—I prefer a turkey gravy mix (follow directions on package). Make 1 pint (16 ounces) of gravy. Use the hot water that you reconstituted the puffball

Dip toast points into the mushroom gravy—or use it as a styptic over a mastodon goring.

in to rehydrate the gravy mix. Add 1½ cups chopped and sautéed oyster or chicken mushrooms, aborted entolomas, or honey mushrooms to the gravy.

Magdalenian Mushrooms
Serves 4

Sauté 2 cups mushrooms de jour in butter and 3 tablespoons minced wild gingerroot (Oriental ginger will work if you don't have access to wild ginger). Cool, stir into sour cream, season with nutmeg (about ½ teaspoon). Use on soups, tacos, burritos, toast points, or as a chip dip—great on a serving of lamb or venison—rich, too; *jawohl, das stimmt*!

Mushroom salsa

Fungal Jim's Morel Mushroom (or Any Other Edible Mushroom) Pâté
Serves 6

1½ ounces dried morel mushrooms (you may also use shiitake or other favorite mushrooms)
1 medium shallot
1 teaspoon garlic, minced finely
1 tablespoon olive oil
2 tablespoons vegetarian oyster sauce
½ cup plain yogurt
½ cup soft tofu
Panko and oil for frying

Preparation: In warm 100°F water, soak dried mushrooms for about 1 hour, or until rehydrated. Squeeze out excess water, then chop fine. Sauté mushrooms, shallots, and garlic in olive oil and oyster sauce.

Process in a blender ½ cup yogurt with ½ cup soft tofu. Fold in the sautéed mushrooms.

Press into a tight, thick triangle, coat with panko, and fry until a crisp skin forms on the surface of the pâté.

Leaky Fry Bread with Prickly Pear Sauce

This is a 2-to-1 mix of bread flour to skim milk. In the Paleolithic tradition, increase the fiber and protein of the fry bread by adding cattail pollen and flaxseeds—1 tablespoon each to 1 cup flour.

SERVES 4

Fry bread with cheese-smothered chorizo taco

Mix 1 cup whole-grain bread flour with slightly less than ½ cup skim milk. Knead the mix on a board sprinkled with flour, folding 20 or so times (to form a moist, firm dough ball). Pluck an egg-size ball from the dough, roll it out on a floured board with a rolling pin until it forms a flat ⅛-inch-thick pancake of dough. Cut a slit or two into the fry bread dough. Place the dough into 400°F oil (canola or peanut). Fry 5 or 6 seconds on each side (until the dough fills with air and browns slightly).

To make prickly pear sauce from the fruit: Press the juice from about 20 fruits (depends on size of fruit) until you have 1 pint. Simmer until thickened slightly; add 1 tablespoon lime juice and ½ cup sugar, stir. Pour hot prickly pear sauce over fry bread.

Tapas-Style Wild Plant Recipes

Once again, substitute what you have available in your area for the following ingredients. These are taste-as-you-go recipes and withstand a great deal of sniffing, handling, and tasting.

Wild Leek and Cheese Stuffed Poblanos (Chiles Rellenos)

SERVES 2

2 large poblano peppers
7 wild leek bulbs, chopped
2 spears wild asparagus, chopped
2 tablespoons chopped Jerusalem artichokes
Olive oil for sautéing
1 teaspoon soy sauce
¼ cup Brie or mild cheddar, grated, plus more for the top
¼ cup chopped fresh cilantro
Egg mixed with 1 teaspoon water
1 cup all-purpose flour
1 cup peanut oil
1 cup mild salsa (or 1 cup chopped fresh tomato)
Sour cream

Preparation: Roast peppers under broiler until skin begins to blacken and bubble; remove to cool. In a 10-inch pan, sauté leeks, asparagus, and artichokes in olive oil and soy sauce. After poblanos cool, pull off skin (I occasionally leave the skin on for fiber). After removing pepper seeds, stuff poblanos with cheese, sautéed vegetables, and raw cilantro. Dip stuffed poblanos in beaten egg and water; place in a plastic bag with flour, and gently roll the poblanos to coat. Fry the

Poblanos stuffed with wild leeks, artichokes, and chopped asparagus

poblanos in ¼ inch of peanut oil; while doing so, pour the leftover beaten egg over top. When the egg hardens, the poblano is done. Sprinkle with cheese, salsa or tomato, and a dollop of sour cream.

Wild Asparagus and Stinging Nettle Crostini
Serves 3–4

1 loaf whole wheat French bread
¼ cup olive oil
½ pound fresh wild asparagus
¼ pound chopped stinging nettle tops
¼ pound finely chopped chickweed (or substitute chopped dandelion leaves)
¼ teaspoon salt
¼ teaspoon pepper
½ cup grated Asiago or Manchego cheese
2 fresh tomatoes, sliced
¼ cup Parmesan cheese

Crostini with stinging nettle

Preparation: Slice bread loaf in half horizontally, brush cut sides with olive oil. Place under preheated broiler for 1 minute; remove.

Cook coarsely chopped asparagus, nettle tops, and chickweed for 2 minutes in ½ inch boiling water. Add salt and pepper to taste. (Makes 2 cups.)

Spread cooked wild vegetables on toasted side of bread. Top with grated cheese and broil for 1 minute, or until cheese melts and bubbles.

Top each crostini with half a slice of tomato, sprinkle with Parmesan, cut, and serve.

Wild Leek, Watercress, and Nettle Pie

SERVES 6

- Cooking spray
- 2 cups chopped whole wild leeks
- Water
- 5 cups chopped watercress
- 2 cups chopped wild violet leaves
- 3 cups fresh arugula
- 5 cups chopped nettles
- 2 cups chopped chickweed
- ¾ cup fresh chopped fennel (bronze preferred)
- ½ cup ricotta cheese
- ½ cup grated elderberry wine cheese (available in gourmet supermarkets—made in Great Britain; if not available, use Fontinella or Asiago)
- ½ cup chopped fresh parsley
- ¼ cup chopped fresh dill (or 2 tablespoons dried dill)
- ½ teaspoon salt
- ½ teaspoon pepper
- 8 sheets phyllo dough, thawed
- 3 tablespoons chopped black walnuts, for garnish

Preparation: Spray the bottom of a 6-quart pan with cooking spray, then sauté chopped leeks until slightly browned. Remove to colander and drain. Spray the pan again and add ½ cup water. Fill the pan with the watercress, violet leaves, arugula, nettle, and chickweed, and simmer until wilted.

Use a colander to press moisture from all the greens, including the leeks. Then in a large mixing bowl, combine the chopped (and uncooked) fennel with the cooked vegetables, the ricotta, and the grated cheese. Mix in parsley, dill, salt, and pepper. Set aside.

Coat each sheet of phyllo dough with cooking spray and press phyllo into a 10-inch (oil-sprayed) pie dish, arranging in a crisscross pattern. Gently press into the bottom and up the sides. Spoon in vegetables and cheese mixture evenly. Fold ends of phyllo dough toward center of the pan, coat ends with cooking spray, and press to seal.

Bake in a preheated 375°F oven for 40 minutes (until golden brown). Sprinkle chopped nuts over and serve.

Watercress and Wild Leek Stir-Fry

SERVES 2 AS A MAIN DISH OR 6 AS TAPAS

Watercress and Wild Leek Stir-Fry

- 4 tablespoons stock (1 tablespoon seasoned rice wine vinegar, 3 tablespoons vegetarian stock)
- 2 tablespoons peanut oil
- 2 tablespoons chopped ginger
- ½ teaspoon brown sugar (optional)
- 3 tablespoons low-salt soy sauce
- 1 teaspoon dark sesame oil
- 6 whole wild leeks, cut lengthwise in half
- 1 bunch watercress (cut away large stems and chop leaves and smaller stems coarsely)
- 2 teaspoons toasted sesame seeds
- 3 tablespoons chopped cilantro

Preparation: Combine stock, peanut oil, ginger, sugar, and soy sauce and swirl until hot in a wok or 12-inch frying pan. Add dark sesame oil and leeks; fry until tender, about 2 minutes. Add chopped watercress and cook for 1 minute. Serve garnished with toasted sesame seeds and cilantro.

Options: Add or substitute chopped stinging nettle and chopped cattail shoots.

Wild Mushrooms with Wild Leeks and Stinging Nettle Enchiladas

SERVES 2 AS A MAIN DISH OR 6 AS TAPAS

Stinging Nettle Enchiladas

- 3 wild leeks, leaf and bulb
- 1 tablespoon olive oil (or canola cooking spray)
- 6 spring morels, chopped
- 3 cups chopped stinging nettle
- 2 tablespoons water
- Salt and pepper to taste
- 5 fresh corn tortillas
- 1 jar mole (white or red)

Preparation: Sauté chopped leeks in olive oil for 1 minute. Add chopped morels, stinging nettle, and water; stir-fry for 2 minutes, until steam wilts the stinging nettle. Salt and pepper to taste. Serve hot inside a rolled tortilla smothered in white or red mole.

Note: Mole can be purchased at a Mexican grocery; follow directions on the jar.

Options: Add watercress to this recipe. Also try with cattail shoots.

Tortilla Española with Morels, Jerusalem Artichokes, and Wild Asparagus

SERVES 6 AS A MAIN DISH, OR 12 AS TAPAS

Tortilla Española

Cooking spray

3 Jerusalem artichokes, sliced ¼ inch thick (enough to cover the bottom of a 10-inch cast iron skillet)

12 asparagus shoots

1 cup sliced roasted green, yellow, and/ or red pepper

½ cup cleaned and coarsely chopped watercress

1½ cups morel mushrooms, sliced (or other edible mushrooms)

Optional addition to frittata: ½ cup thinly sliced burdock root

6 whole eggs

1 teaspoon Lawry's salt (or equivalent of salt and pepper)

3 tablespoons fresh chopped cilantro

¼ cup grated Parmesan cheese

5–6 corn tortillas

Salsa or pico de gallo (see optional recipe)

1 can refried beans

Preparation: Preheat oven to 350°F. Spray the bottom of a cast-iron skillet with nonstick oil. Arrange slices of Jerusalem artichokes across the bottom of the pan, forming a base. Place asparagus shoots on the artichokes like the spokes of a wheel. Spread roasted peppers over the first 2 layers, then add a thin layer of chopped watercress and mushrooms. Whip the eggs, salt, pepper, and chopped cilantro into a froth. Slowly pour the airy mix of eggs over the layers of vegetables in the skillet. Sprinkle the top liberally with Parmesan cheese. Cook for 15 minutes in the heated oven, then brown the top for about 1 minute under the broiler. Cut like a quiche and serve over a corn tortilla with salsa and refried beans.

Optional: Pico de gallo is simple to make: Chop 1 ripe tomato; add ½ small onion, diced, ½ jalapeño pepper, diced, 2 tablespoons chopped cilantro, and the juice of ½ lime. Mix all with a fork. Salt and pepper to taste. Garnish lavishly over frittata.

Divorced* Eggs with Morels and Wild Leek (Ramps) Leaves

SERVES 1

- 2 tablespoons finely chopped wild leek leaves
- 2 tablespoons minced watercress
- 1 morel, chopped
- 1 tablespoon butter
- Salt and pepper
- 3 tablespoons green salsa (recipe below)
- 3 tablespoons red salsa (recipe below)
- 2 eggs
- 1 corn tortilla
- 1 teaspoon chopped cilantro
- ½ cup refried black beans

Preparation: Sauté chopped leek leaves, watercress, and morel in butter for 2 minutes. Salt and pepper to taste. Warm both salsas in the microwave separately (do not mix). Divide chopped leeks and morels and add to each salsa in equal amounts. Cook 2 eggs over easy. Pour green salsa over one egg and red salsa over the other. Serve over an oil fried corn tortilla, garnish with cilantro, and serve with a side of refried beans.

Red salsa recipe: Combine 1 cup chopped fresh tomatoes, 1 cup chopped onions, and ½ jalapeño pepper, minced. Add juice of ½ lime, 3 wild leek bulbs, minced, and 1 tablespoon chopped cilantro. Salt and pepper to taste.

Green salsa recipe: Boil 6 whole peeled tomatillos in water until tender, about 5 minutes. Cool tomatillos in ice water. Blend tomatillos with ½ cup chopped sweet onion using a countertop electric blender. Add ½ jalapeño pepper, minced (optional), and juice of ¼ lime. Salt and pepper to taste.

*Red salsa represents passion and anger; green salsa is for naïveté or inexperience—the colors of a failed marriage. This is a traditional Yucatecan breakfast.

Vegetarian Beans with Wild Greens in Spring Stock

SERVES 4

- 1 cup chopped watercress
- ½ cup chopped stinging nettle
- ½ cup mushrooms of your choice (try oysters)
- ½ cup chopped violet leaves
- 2 quarts water
- 1 clove garlic, chopped
- 1 (16-ounce) can black beans
- 1 can (16-ounce) pinto beans
- Sprig of epazote (optional)
- Juice of 1 lime
- 1 teaspoon each dried oregano and dried basil
- Soy sauce or salt and pepper to taste
- ½ cup fresh chickweed
- ½ cup dandelion petals
- 2 tablespoons chopped rosemary

Vegetarian Beans and Wild Greens

Preparation: Combine all ingredients except the chickweed, dandelion petals, and rosemary in a saucepan with 2 quarts water. Bring to a boil; back off to a simmer for 15 minutes. Strain off the liquid and reserve the stock for soup, stir-fries, or anywhere vegetable-flavored water will enhance the dish.

Finally, stir the chickweed and dandelion petals into the greens-and-beans mixture; garnish with rosemary and serve.

Wild Plants and Morel Vegetarian Lasagna

SERVES 4

- ½ cup cottage cheese
- 1 cup grated Parmesan cheese, plus more for garnish
- ½ cup ricotta
- 8 morel mushrooms, coarsely chopped
- 2 cups chopped stinging nettle
- ½ cup chopped wild leeks
- 1 cup finely chopped wild asparagus (domestic variety is OK)
- 1 cup milk
- ½ cup water
- ½ teaspoon each dried parsley, thyme, chervil, oregano, and basil
- 3 cloves garlic, finely chopped
- 1 (14- to 16-ounce) can tomato sauce
- 1 pound un-boiled spinach lasagna noodles
- Chopped flat-leaf Italian parsley, for garnish

Preparation: In a bowl, combine the cheeses, wild ingredients, and milk. In a separate bowl, combine the dry seasonings and garlic with the tomato sauce and ½ cup water. To start, ladle ½ cup of sauce on the bottom of a lasagna dish. Then put down a layer of noodles. Top that layer of noodles with ⅓ of the sauce and then a layer of the milk, cheese, vegetable mix. Repeat the layering twice more: noodles, red sauce, white sauce. You have three layers of noodles. Four is typical, three is good enough. Top the last layer with ¼ cup Parmesan.

Bake, covered, in a preheated 325°F oven for 55 minutes, until noodles are soft. Cool. Garnish with more Parmesan cheese and chopped Italian parsley.

Wild Leeks with Anchovies in Mesclun Salad

SERVES 6–8

Buried leeks surprise

> 30 wild leeks tops, cut into 4-inch
>   lengths
> Unsalted butter
> 5 anchovies, soaked several times in
>   fresh water to release salt
> ¼ cup chopped parsley
> Mesclun salad mix
> 1 tablespoon chopped lovage (or 3
>   tablespoons chopped parsley)
> 1 teaspoon minced chives
> Sliced fresh tomatoes
> 3 avocados, sliced
> ¼ cup grated sharp cheese
> ¾ cup blue cheese

Vinaigrette
Juice of 1 lemon
1 teaspoon minced chives (preferably) or wild onion tops
Salt and pepper
¼ cup olive oil
1 tablespoon finely chopped lovage (or 3 tablespoons chopped parsley)

Leeks and Anchovies: Sauté the leeks in butter until tender (about 2 minutes). Meanwhile, combine the vinaigrette ingredients while the leeks cook and cool. Cut the anchovies into small bits. Spread the cold leeks on a plate, drizzle with vinaigrette, and garnish with finely chopped anchovies and parsley. Bury leeks under mesclun mix, lovage or parsley, chives, sliced tomatoes, and avocado slices. Garnish with grated sharp cheese and blue cheese; serve.

Vegetarian Egg Roll with Wild Berries and Maple Syrup Salsa

SERVES 3–4

Vegetarian Egg Roll, shown here with Mexican white sauce (mayo, sour cream, and cilantro to taste)

¼ cup Riesling wine

3 tablespoons maple syrup

½ cup blueberries, raspberries, blackberries, and/or autumn olives, in combination or by themselves (or substitute any other wild berry)

¼ cup dried elderberries

2 tablespoons lemon juice

1 tablespoon Dijon mustard

1 tablespoon soy sauce

1 tablespoon sesame seed oil

12 prepared vegetarian egg rolls or pot stickers

Preparation: Mix the wine, syrup, lemon juice, mustard, and soy sauce in a saucepan. Bring to a boil, then simmer and reduce; add the berries, mash and cook until thickened. Remove from heat and stir the sesame seed oil into the finished salsa. Prepare egg rolls or pot stickers as directed. Use the maple syrup salsa as dip, or drizzle it over egg rolls or pot stickers.

Miso Burdock Soup with a Nasturtium Flower Garnish

SERVES 1

Burdock miso soup

Miso soup base

Vegetable bouillon cube or vegetable stock

1 burdock root

1 cup watercress

Sour cream

2 nasturtium flowers, for garnish

Fennel fronds, for garnish

Preparation: Prepare this soup according to your taste for miso. I like using the lighter white miso mix, about 1 tablespoon to 1 cup stock. Peel and slice the burdock root thinly (⅛ inch). Simmer the miso and burdock root for 10 minutes. Drop in a sprig or two of watercress for each cup. Simmer for 2 minutes. Serve with a dollop of sour cream; garnish each bowl with 2 nasturtium blossoms and a feather of fennel leaf.

Marinated Rabbit with Sliced Prickly Pear Cactus Pads

SERVES 2–4

¼ cup reduced sodium soy sauce
5 juniper berries, crushed
¼ cup red wine (Cabernet or Burgundy)
½ teaspoon minced rosemary
1 tablespoon minced gingerroot (wild American or Oriental)
¼ teaspoon herbes de Provence (optional)
1 rabbit, quartered (3–4 pounds dressed)
1 cup apple juice
½ cup beef broth
Panko bread crumbs
Salt and pepper
2 egg yolks
½ teaspoon pepper
3 tablespoons flour
4 cups prickly pear cactus pads, skinned and thorns removed
Peanut oil, for frying

Juniper and soy–marinated rabbit with sliced prickly pear pads

Preparation: In a large ziplock bag, combine soy sauce, crushed juniper berries, red wine, rosemary, gingerroot, and, if desired, herbes de Provence. Place the rabbit parts in the marinade and refrigerate for at least 4 hours and up to 6, shaking the bag every 2 hours.

Remove the rabbit from the ziplock bag and pour the marinade into a roasting pan. Add the apple juice and beef broth to the marinade. Shake the rabbit in a bag with the panko coating and add salt and pepper to taste. Place the rabbit in the pan and roast at 350°F for 1 hour, until brown and tender, basting occasionally to keep it moist. The marinade may be reduced to make a sauce.

While rabbit is roasting: Beat the egg yolks in a bowl, stirring in the pepper and flour. Coat the cactus pads in the batter and fry in a pan of peanut oil (about ½ inch oil) until brown on all sides.

Serve: Serve rabbit with prickly pear pads and optional roasted vegetables (see below). Marinade is reduced and used as a sauce.

Option: Roast chunked root vegetables in the last hour with the rabbit: potato, sweet potato, rutabaga, parsnip, and onion.

Jerusalem Artichoke Shoot Tempura

Break off early spring shoots of Jerusalem artichokes before the leaves open. Whip an egg (or just an egg white); dip shoots in the egg, drop them in a ziplock bag of rice or wheat flour, shake, coat, and sauté or deep-fry until golden.

Persimmon Pudding
Serves 6

    1 cup persimmon pulp

    1 cup sugar

    3 eggs, beaten

    1 cup whole wheat flour

    1 teaspoon baking powder

    ½ teaspoon cinnamon

    ½ teaspoon nutmeg

    ¼ pound butter, softened

    1 cup milk

    ¼ cup black walnuts

    ¼ cup hickory nuts

Preparation: Combine persimmon pulp with sugar in a bowl; beat in the eggs. In a separate bowl, mix the flour and baking powder with cinnamon, nutmeg, butter, and milk. Stir this mixture and the nuts into the persimmon base. Pour into a well-greased 9-inch cake pan. Bake at 325°F for 35 minutes.

Italian Cream Cake with Hazelnuts, Black Walnuts, Blackberries, Strawberries, and Blueberries
Serves 8

Italian Cream Cake

Note: all ingredients should be at room temperature

    5 eggs, separated

    1 cup butter, softened

    1¾ cups sugar

    2 cups white flour

    ½ teaspoon baking soda

    ½ teaspoon salt

    1 cup black walnuts, chopped

    ½ cup chopped hazelnuts

    ¾ cup coconut

    1 teaspoon vanilla

    1⅛ cups sour milk (or buttermilk)

    ½ cup each as garnish: blueberries, blackberries, and strawberries

To make the cake: Preheat oven to 350°F. Lightly grease and flour two 9-inch round cake pans. Separate the eggs. Beat the whites until soft peaks form; set aside. Cream the egg yolks, butter, and sugar; set aside. Take 2 bowls—one for the dry ingredients and a smaller bowl or tiny pitcher for the milk and vanilla. In the bigger bowl combine the dry ingredients—flour, baking soda, salt, nuts, and coconut. In the smaller bowl (or pitcher), add the vanilla to the sour milk or buttermilk (whatever you choose). Alternate adding the dry ingredients and the milk ingredients to the egg/butter/sugar you creamed together.

Now, fold in the egg whites. Pour the batter into prepared pans. Bake for about 20 to 25 minutes. Do the basic toothpick test to be sure they're done. When cool, slice each layer into two thinner layers.

The frosting: 4 cups powdered sugar (sift it if lumpy!), 1 cup butter, 4 ounces softened cream cheese, ½ teaspoon vanilla, 1 tablespoon rum (optional), ½ cup orange marmalade (optional).

Frosting procedure: Slowly blend all ingredients except for the orange marmalade. After blended, beat the mixture on high setting until light and fluffy. Apply frosting to the cake with frosting spatula. Then, if desired, heat the orange marmalade so it will flow in a cup or pitcher so you can pour it out slowly. For the middle layer, drizzle orange marmalade over the frosting. If you want to drizzle it on top, try warming it more; it will then be "drizzly"-looking instead of clumpy. Garnish with berries.

Compliments to Bill Fields.

Dried Salal Berry Cakes
Salal berries were an important traditional food of Native Americans of the Northwest. They gathered the berries and prepared them in cakes.
SERVES 10

To make a fair facsimile of a dried cake, boil 8 cups berries until they are a soft mash, and then pour them into a greased cupcake pan, filling each cupcake compartment half full. Bake at 200°F until the cakes dry, about 3½ hours. Reconstitute dried cakes by soaking them in water overnight in the refrigerator.

Rabbit Stew with Juniper
SERVES 4
- 5 juniper berries, crushed
- 3 cups chicken broth
- 3 tablespoons soy sauce
- 2 tablespoons dried and powdered puffball mushroom
- ¼ cup Riesling wine
- 1 whole rabbit (halved or quartered)
- Wild root vegetables: 3 Jerusalem artichokes, 6 whole leeks, 2 burdock roots, cubed

Rabbit Stew with Juniper

Preparation: Boil the juniper berries, broth, soy sauce, puffball mushroom powder, and wine in a stockpot. Sauté the rabbit, add it to the stock and stew for 30 minutes. Add wild veggies—Jerusalem artichokes, wild leeks, and cubed burdock roots—during the last 10 minutes.

Hazelnut-Encrusted Chicken Breast with Raspberry Sauce

SERVES 2

For the Chicken:

1 cup ground hazelnuts

1 cup panko (Japanese bread crumbs)

2 chicken breasts

1 cup peanut oil

For the Sauce:

¾ cup raspberries

3 tablespoons white wine vinegar

1 tablespoon sugar

½ cup safflower oil

3–6 teaspoons water

Hazelnut-Encrusted Chicken Breast

Preparation: Combine the hazelnuts and panko in a bowl. Coat the chicken in the mixture and fry the chicken in the peanut oil.

Simmer the raspberries, vinegar, sugar, safflower oil, and water in a saucepan. Reduce to thickness of motor oil. Serve over the chicken and enjoy.

Crab Cakes with Wild Leeks

SERVES 4–6

1 pound blue crab meat (or Dungeness, rock, king, or other crabmeat or a mixture)

8 saltine crackers

1 egg, beaten

2 tablespoons mayonnaise

1 teaspoon mustard

¼ teaspoon Worcestershire sauce

½ teaspoon Old Bay seasoning

10 wild leeks, finely chopped

Salt to taste

2 tablespoons vegetable oil

Juice of 1 lime (or 6 slices of lime)

Jewelweed shoots (optional)

Crab cake with chopped leeks and jewelweed shoots

Preparation: Put the crabmeat in a bowl and set it aside. Finely crush the crackers and mix them with the next 7 ingredients (egg through salt). Gently fold in the crab; don't break up the crab into fine shreds. Shape 6 crab cakes, and refrigerate them for at least 1 hour. Then heat the oil in a nonstick frying pan. Sauté the crab cakes until golden brown on each side, 3 to 5 minutes per side. Squeeze on lime juice, or garnish with lime slices or jewelweed shoots.

Appendix C: References and Resources

DVDs

Jim Meuninck has produced several 2-hour videos that identify and demonstrate the use of edible and medicinal wild plants. For useful information, go to Jim Meuninck YouTube to view these free videos.

Cooking with Edible Flowers and Culinary Herbs. Jim Meuninck and Sinclair Philip (Jim Meuninck YouTube).

Diet for Natural Health. Jim Meuninck, Candace Corson, MD, and Nancy Behnke Strasser, RD (Jim Meuninck YouTube). One diet for both disease prevention and weight control.

Edible Wild Plants IV. Jim Meuninck and Dr. Jim Duke (Jim Meuninck YouTube). More than 100 useful wild herbs documented, recipes demonstrated.

Native American Medicine. Jim Meuninck, Patsy Clark, Estela Roman, and Theresa Barnes (Jim Meuninck YouTube).

Natural Health with Medicine Herbs and Healing Foods. Jim Meuninck, Ed Smith, and James Balch (Jim Meuninck YouTube).

Survival X. Jim Meuninck (Jim Meuninck YouTube). Self-reliance and survival skills demonstrated.

Websites

Join Jim on Facebook and Jim Meuninck YouTube. See and order his field guides, audiobooks, memoir, and fiction at his blog: Jim Meuninck Amazon.

Mushroom web resources:

mushroomexpert.com

mycokey.com

mycology.cornell.edupsms.org

mushroomworld.com.sg

Edible wild plants resources:

pacificbotanicals.com

ediblewildfood.com

wildedible.com

ediblewildplants.com

wildmanstevebrill.com

Books

The Audubon Field Guide to North American Wild Flowers. New York: Alfred Knopf, Chanticleer Press Edition, 1992.

Barnes, Burton, and Warren Wagner Jr. *Michigan Trees,* rev. and updated. Ann Arbor, MI: University of Michigan Press, 2004.

Duke, James A. *Handbook of Edible Weeds.* Boca Raton, FL: CRC Press, 2001.

———. *Handbook of Medicinal Herbs.* Boca Raton, FL: CRC Press, 2001.

———. *Handbook of Northeastern Indian Medicinal Plants.* Lincoln, MA: Quarterman Publications, 1986.

———. *Handbook of Nuts.* Boca Raton, FL: CRC Press, 2001.

Elias, Thomas, and Peter Dykeman. *Field Guide to North American Edible Wild Plants.* New York: Van Nostrand Reinhold, 1982.

Forey, Pamela, and Cecilia Fitzsimons. *An Instant Guide to Edible Plants.* Gramercy Books, 2001.

Foster, Steven, and James Duke. *Field Guide to Medicinal Plants and Herbs of Eastern and Central North America* (Peterson Field Guides), 2nd ed. New York: Houghton Mifflin, 2000.

Kershaw, Linda. *Edible and Medicinal Plants of the Rockies.* Auburn, WA: Lone Pine Publishing, 2004.

Kindscher, Kelly. *Medicinal Wild Plants of the Prairie.* Lawrence: University Press of Kansas, 1992.

McConnaughey, Evelyn. *Sea Vegetables.* Happy Camp, CA: Naturegraph Publishers, 1985.

Meuninck, Jim. *Medicinal Plants of North America: A Field Guide.* Guilford, CT: FalconGuides, 2016.

Moerman, Daniel. *Native American Ethnobotany.* Portland, OR: Timber Press, 1998.

Tilford, Gregory. *Edible and Medicinal Plants of the West.* Missoula, MT: Mountain Press Publishing, 1997.

Whitney, Stephen. *Western Forests.* New York: Alfred A. Knopf, 1985.

Recipe Index

Index

About the Author

Jim Meuninck, biologist, naturalist, writer, and lecturer, has authored six Falcon Guides and fourteen special-interest DVDs on edible wild plants, Native American medicine, medicinal plants, self-reliance and survival, and alternative health. Now residing in Michigan, he has lived in four countries, documenting indigenous food and culture on three continents. His favorite pastimes are traveling, reading, fly fishing, canoeing, trekking, biking, and

Jim Meuninck

camping. His spouse, Jill, joins Jim on foraging forays, and his daughter, Rebecca Meuninck, PhD in anthropology, shares time with her parents in remote wilderness areas. Jim's DVDs may be seen at Jim Meuninck YouTube. His Falcon Guides include *Medicinal Plants of North America*, *Foraging Mushrooms Oregon*, *Basic Illustrated Edible and Medicinal Mushrooms*, *Basic Illustrated Poisonous and Psychoactive Plants*, *Basic Illustrated Medicinal Plants*, and *Foraging Mushrooms Washington*. He has also authored two novels and a memoir: *Into the Haze, Montana Dog,* and *The Angel and the Atheist*. Join Jim on Facebook.